Physical Characteristics of the Briard
(from The Kennel Club breed standard)

Body: Back firm and level, chest broad, medium spring of rib, well let down, very slight slope at croup, determining set of tail. Very slightly longer in body than height at shoulder.

Hindquarters: Well angulated, with hocks set not too low and turning neither in nor out, but leg below hock not quite vertical. Hindlegs, particularly thighs, well muscled. Double dewclaws set low on hindlegs of utmost importance.

Tail: Long, well covered with hair with upward hook at tip. Carried low but always held centrally. Bone of tail reaching at least point of hock.

Colour: All black, or with white hairs scattered through black coat. Fawn or slate grey.

Feet: Strong, turning neither in nor out, slightly rounded, about midway between cat foot and hare foot. Well covered with hair.

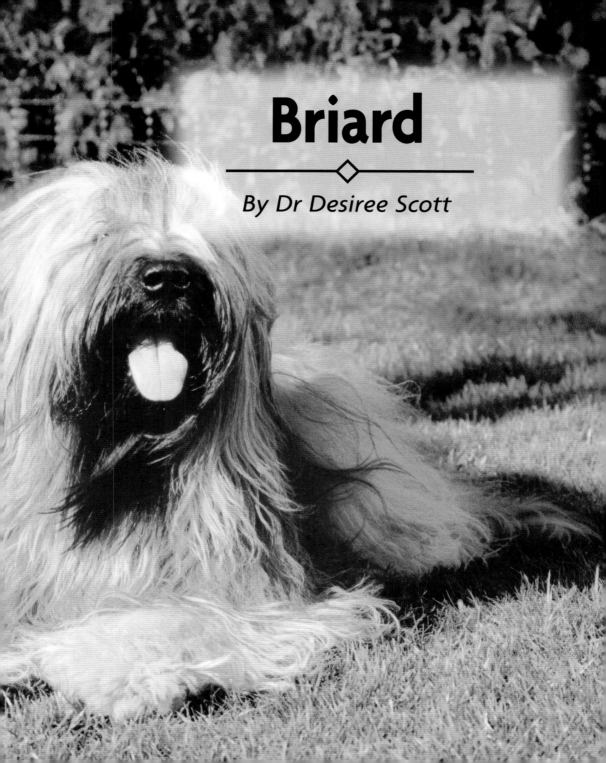

Briard

By Dr Desiree Scott

CONTENTS

PUBLISHED IN THE UNITED KINGDOM BY:

INTERPET
PUBLISHING
Vincent Lane, Dorking, Surrey RH4 3YX England

ISBN 1-903098-84-X

Photography by Isabelle Français, Carol Ann Johnson, Dr Desiree Scott and Michael Trafford with additional photography by
Norvia Behling, TJ Calhoun, Carolina Biological Supply, David Dalton, Doskocil, Katri and Markku Espo, James Hayden-Yoav, James R Hayden, RBP, Bill Jonas, Dwight R Kuhn, Dr Dennis Kunkel, M Marks, Mikki Pet Products, Phototake, Jamie Putnam, Jean Claude Revy, Dr Andrew Spielman, Chuck Tatham and Alice van Kempen.

Illustrations by Dr Desiree Scott.

The publisher wishes to thank all of the owners whose dogs are featured in this book.

BRIARD

The bearded Briard derives from France, where the breed was used as a livestock guardian and herding dog. The breed's beard is one of its distinctive features, as is the feathering on its ears, which are never cropped in the UK but are frequently seen cropped in the US and on the Continent.

The Briard is one of a large group of European sheepdogs characterised by the hair on their chins that form beards. Briards come from France, and their hairy relatives stretch from the Balkans to Scotland.

The Briard is a sheepdog that descends from an ancient type of dog called the livestock guardian. Livestock guardians work with sheep in a protective way; the Briard and its smooth-coated relation, the Beauceron, are more recent types that can be used to move sheep as well as guard them.

Notice that I do not use the word 'breed' when referring to dogs of long ago. There was no such thing as a breed of dog until the mid-19th century, when the Victorians invented dog shows and the differently shaped dogs were formally classified for the first time. Until this time, there were only different dog types.

DOMESTICATION AND CLASSIFICATION

Domestication was a way of life chosen by those animals that have now become domesticated species, because it was an easier way to live. Our dogs are

THE STORY OF THE CHIEN D'AUBREY

There are several romantic stories concerning how the Briard got its name. It is not connected in a specific way to the French area of Brie (from where the cheese comes), and it has been said that 'Briard' is a corruption of the name 'Chien d'Aubrey.' Sir Aubrey de Montdidier was a French aristocrat who was murdered in 1371 in front of his Briard. Every time the dog came across the assassin, the dog became enraged and tried to attack the killer. The King of France ordered that a duel should take place between the dog and the accused, a man named Richard de Macaire. The dog was the victor, and Macaire confessed and was beheaded.

provided with food, shelter, medical care and many other extras. In the past, human support was not as comprehensive as that which the modern pet now receives, but the rubbish dumps of the first human settlements were easy places for dogs to rifle for scraps. Those dogs that were the least afraid of people fared the best, for it was a real waste of energy to run away all the time.

Furthermore, if the dogs could have their puppies near the rubbish dumps, which were the food sources, they conserved the energy that would have been used by trailing back to the den with food. Once the more sentimental members of the human communities saw the puppies, people started to have a direct effect on domestication by giving extra protection to the most people-friendly puppies.

Once sheep were domesticated, selection pressure was put on the village dogs, thus separating them into the two earliest dog types: the sheep-friendly livestock guardians and the sighthounds, which retained their adult killing behaviour patterns.

The earliest dog breeders did not choose their dogs because of their appearance but because of their behaviour patterns. The reason that livestock guardians are safe with domestic livestock is that they retain the behaviour patterns of puppies and remain at the 'play' stage all their lives. They retain the juvenile appearance traits of floppy ears, big heads and facial wrinkles that the sighthound puppy soon outgrows.

The dogs that were not livestock guardians, the ones that were not livestock-friendly because they displayed their full adult behaviour patterns, were retained because of their hunting prowess; these were the sighthounds.

Although shepherding is not as popular in the 21st century as it was in past centuries, the Briard still serves in this capacity for European farmers.

SPREAD OF THE LIVESTOCK GUARDIANS

The livestock guardians and the sighthounds first developed in the area where farming and the domestication of sheep originated. Recent DNA analyses on domesticated wheat have traced this back to the southeastern border of Turkey, next to Iraq. It is from this area that both of these types of dog spread, with other domesticated animals (goats and cattle), both east and west. Going east, they arrived in Tibet and China, which is exactly the reverse of what most dog books say. The books do not give any explanation of how a farming dog spontaneously appeared in an area where agriculture came much later. The Tibetan Mastiff is the livestock guardian of the Himalayas, but it is derived from the dogs of the Near East—how could it be the ancestor of dogs developed in Turkey many hundreds of years before?

France, however, is in the opposite direction of Tibet, and we have to follow the spread of farming into Europe from the Near East during the Neolithic, or New Stone, Age. The reason that archaeologists gave names such as 'Stone Age' and 'Iron Age' is that when serious studies of these eras began, there were no techniques with which to work out exact dates; thus, the period of time before metal implements were used was called the Stone Age. Even so, the axes and other tools made from stone were highly polished to make sharp blades and were very effective. The main problem with them was that they could not last as long as the metal tools that were to follow.

The actual date of the Neolithic Age alters in different places, for the change to farming occurred in the Near East before moving through Turkey, into the Balkans and Greece, then along the rivers of Europe to the Atlantic coast of France by about

GENUS *CANIS*

Dogs and wolves are members of the genus *Canis*. Wolves are known scientifically as *Canis lupus* while dogs are known as *Canis familiaris*. The term 'canine' derives from the Latin word for dog, while the word 'dog' itself has a more northerly origin. The German *dogge* and the French *dogue* both mean 'mastiff,' and it is known that in Roman times Britain was famed for its dogs of mastiff type.

BRAIN AND BRAWN

Since dogs have been inbred for centuries, their physical and mental characteristics are constantly being changed to suit man's desires for hunting, retrieving, scenting, guarding and warming their masters' laps. During the past 150 years, dogs have been judged according to physical characteristics as well as functional abilities. Few breeds can boast a genuine balance between physique, working ability and temperament.

5500–4700 BC, crossing into Britain sometime after 4500 BC.

We can plot livestock guardians across Europe. The first places that were farmed were those that had the best soil—the areas next to rivers—and the last areas to be farmed were the poor soils of mountains. However, since that time farming techniques have advanced in the lowland areas, and it is now only in the mountains that the old ways of looking after sheep are still used. This means that many of the remnant populations of livestock guardians are found in mountain ranges, and are called 'Mountain Dogs' by us. Examples of these livestock guardians are the Pyrenean Mountain Dog (called Great Pyrenees in the USA), the Estrela Mountain Dog of Portugal and the Bernese Mountain Dog.

WOLF VS DOG

The latest work on the behaviour patterns of dogs and wolves makes it seem unlikely that the wolf was the immediate ancestor of the dog. This fits in with genetic evidence that the two species split 100,000 years ago. What seems likely is that 100,000 years ago the wolf and dog separated and were two different species, with different behaviour patterns, but the fossil records cannot tell them apart. This would leave the field clear for the much more social dog to have linked up with humans 10,000 years ago, while the wolf to this day cannot be domesticated.

If we look at the map showing how farming spread, we can see how the major rivers were important in spreading this way of life. And if we look at the livestock guardians of Greece, the former Yugoslavia and Romania,

From the turn of the past century, this is how the Briard looked in around 1900.

The smooth-coated relative to the Briard, the Beauceron is gaining recognition around the world as a competent guard dog and protector.

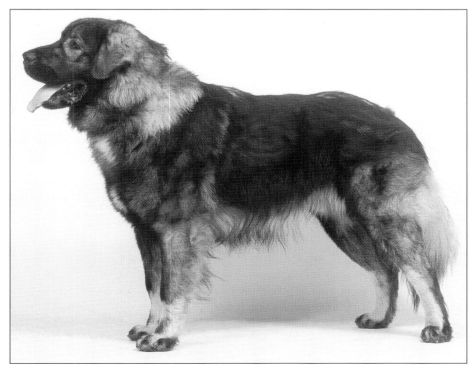

Above: Dogs from Turkey. On the right is a Saluki-type sighthound. The dog on the left is the livestock guardian type that we know as an Anatolian Shepherd Dog.

The Sarplaninac is a livestock guardian dog from the former Yugoslavia.

Above left: The Maremma Sheepdog from Italy is gaining popularity in the UK and elsewhere beyond Continental Europe.
Above right: A very different livestock guardian with its hairy face. This herder derives from Romania.
Right: The Spanish Mastiff, known in Spain as el Mastin Español, is a powerful, impressive flock guardian with a smooth coat.
Below left: The Catalan Sheepdog, known in its native Catalunya as Gos d'Atura, is a versatile herding dog with great promise as a companion and working dog.
Below right: The Portuguese Sheepdog, or Caõ da Serra de Aires, is a working dog that is rarely seen at dog shows.

The bearded Komondor comes from Hungary and is known for its white corded coat and great size.

The Bergamasco Sheepdog of Italy is smaller than the Komondor and possesses a fully-flocked coloured coat, distinguishing it from all other breeds.

The Polish Lowland Sheepdog, or PON, the acronym deriving from its Polish name (Polski Owczarek Nizinny), is one of the furry-faced herding dogs from Europe.

we see a close similarity. These dogs are almost unchanged from their original form because there is only a very short history of dog shows in these countries. With the coming of dog-show competition, dog breeders have altered the appearance of many breeds to make them more 'glamorous.'

THE BEARDED SHEEPDOGS
Long-distance trading took place long before the first use of metals, and one of the areas in which the greatest markets took place was

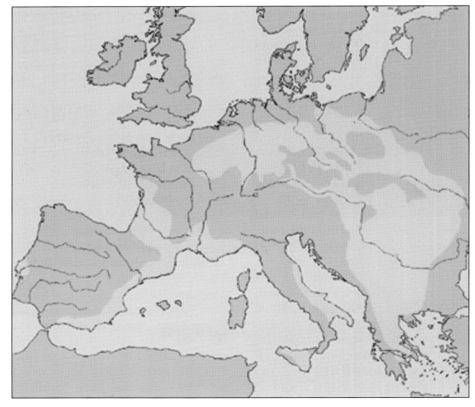

the Carpathian Basin, an area that is now part of Hungary and Romania. If we plot the geographical origin of all of today's livestock guardians, we find a new type of dog appearing here—the livestock guardian with a beard. In Hungary it is the Komondor and in Romania the very similar Mioritic Sheepdog, with the South Russian Ovtcharka found in the southeastern republics that used to be part of the Soviet Union.

The 'bearded' sheepdogs extended over Europe to the Bearded Collie of Scotland and to the east to the Kyi Apso of Tibet. The Kyi Apso is similar to the Tibetan Mastiff, with a coat like that of a scruffy Lhasa Apso.

SHEEPDOGS OF FRANCE

France has many native breeds, and among these are five sheepdog breeds that are internationally recognised. There are a number of unrecognised types from the South of France as well, but these are not as yet being selectively bred. The Picardy Sheepdog belongs to the German/Belgian/Dutch Shepherd Dog complex, but the others are more closely related to each other.

The Briard is the large hairy French sheepdog, while the Beauceron is the smooth version. The Pyrenean Sheepdog is the small hairy type, with the Smooth-faced Pyrenean Sheepdog

The Pyrenean Sheepdog from France, known there as le Berger des Pyrenees, is a herding dog that comes in three coat styles, long, 'goat' and smooth-faced.

less hairy, but not completely smooth-coated.

When the first dog show was held in Paris in 1863, there were a dozen French sheepdogs entered, of diverse shape and size. The most numerous were dogs of a smooth-haired breed, black and tan in colour, the breed that is now known as the Beauceron. There were also two representatives of the hairy sheepdog known as the Briard. The first Briard was registered in the French Stud Book in 1885, and the first Beauceron in 1893. The Beauceron and the Briard were

Male and female Pyrenean Sheepdogs with a puppy. As companions, these are delightful, happy dogs to share one's life with.

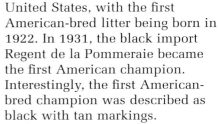

not officially separated until 1896. The Picardy Sheepdog only received recognition in 1922, and the Pyrenean Sheepdog in 1926.

The complex matter of the Briard's colour can only be understood by considering its shared origin with the black and tan Beauceron. This is why bicolour is unacceptable in the Briard, as it demonstrated a Beauceron too near in the pedigree at the time when the two breeds were regularly crossed.

WAR WORKERS

During the First World War, Briards were considered exceptional at locating the injured in the terrible conditions of the mud-caked trenches. Dogs would have to swim rather than walk because of the mud, and it was said that they could tell the difference between someone who had been killed and someone with only a spark of life left, for whom they alerted the attention of the stretcher bearer.

EFFECTS OF WAR ON THE BRIARD

Once the First World War began, the Briard found another job working at the French front line. When the United States joined this war, just at its end, the American soldiers were able to see this large dog in action. They must have been impressed, for the breed was taken back to the

United States, with the first American-bred litter being born in 1922. In 1931, the black import Regent de la Pommeraie became the first American champion. Interestingly, the first American-bred champion was described as black with tan markings.

There had been a French breed club set up just before the First World War, but with the German invasion in 1914 such activities were stopped. The club was reformed in 1924, but the whole of France had to undergo an even more horrific occupation in 1940 when the Nazis invaded. This almost destroyed every facet of French life. There was a puppet government set up by the Germans, but the free French fled to Britain to plan for liberation of their country, leaving those who formed the resistance to hide their activities as best they could. There was little time for breeding dogs; there was even less time for the keeping of accurate pedigrees.

The Briard survived the war in a much healthier state than the Beauceron, but many were requisitioned as army guard dogs. The Beauceron gene pool was greatly depleted and faults that had not been problems before the war recurred—pale eyes, missing teeth and lack of conformation and type. Popularity had shifted, and the Briard was now much more numerous than the smooth-haired Beauceron.

A WORD ABOUT DOG SHOWS

In Europe, the emphasis for dog breeders is slightly different than it is in Britain and the United States. As well as placing the dogs at shows, the judge also grades the dog on how typical it is of the breed, with the top grade being excellent. All of the prizewinners have to have been graded excellent; if no dog of this quality is present, then no prizes are awarded.

The largest show for one breed in the world is the annual German Seiger show for the German Shepherd Dog, where there is an entry of 2000 or so dogs. In the class for adult males, there are more than 150 entered and every dog is graded, even if it comes in last place. Out of these, only 10 or so are graded excellent; thus, going home with a grade of excellent from a show like this is an award of great importance... much more so than the group placements that some American and British people chase after, and where only first over any other dog will do.

The French Briard equivalent of the Seiger show is the Rassemblement, and this was first held in 1970. In 1983, 900 Briards were entered, with 11 dogs and 11 bitches graded excellent. Again, all of the entries are evaluated, and temperament and working ability are considered as well as conformation. The Briard Club of America holds a North American Rassemblement every four years, producing a book with photos of each dog with its pedigree and the point-by point-evaluation, the most wonderful piece of information for choosing Briard parents.

THE BRIARD COMES TO BRITAIN

The Briard came to Britain in 1966 when Nancy Tomlin went to Ireland to join her husband Mike, who was working with a film crew. They had been thinking of a puppy, and the idea of an Irish Wolfhound appealed to them. They went to visit a large multiple-breed kennel called Shannon Kennels, which had been set up by an American with a view to exporting to the American market. Though this was a commercial set-up, the foundation stock that had been chosen was of good quality. Indeed, when the kennel folded in 1968, many of the Briards there found their way to Britain and are behind the British show population.

During the visit to Shannon Kennels in 1966, Mrs Tomlin fell in love with a bouncy black four-month-old Briard called Hubert and brought him home to London. Soon the British canine press, and the general press as well, had pictures of this black hairy dog, the likes of which had never been seen before. He was soon joined at the Tomlins' by his half-sister

MADEMOISELLE TURGIS

The first winner of a British Challenge Certificate was the French import Desamee Tripot de Vasouy, bred by Mademoiselle Turgis in her chateau in Honfleur, Normandy. Apparently the chateau was filled with priceless antiques as well as Briards of a special rich hue of fawn. During the German occupation of France in the 1940s, she worked for the French resistance, hiding British servicemen on her estate. This was a fairly safe place to be, as the Germans were afraid of the Briards that roamed around her walled garden. On the rare occasions that they came to search the chateau, Mme Turgis would call out the names of dogs, using fictitious names so that the servicemen would know to climb out the window and hide in the woods.

Her mode of transport was a cart pulled by two Briards, and with this she smuggled the extra food rations she needed for her secret guests. It was generally a successful mode of transport; however, on one occasion a young Briard saw a cat in a shop window and started to chase it, bringing the cart, its owner and the other Briard with him. The servicemen did manage to get back to England and, as a gesture of thanks after the war, their officer gave Mme Turgis a little car.

Maudie. Soon Mr and Mrs Trueman, who ran the local training classes, had Briards too; they had Maudie's parents brought over from Ireland.

The Tomlins registered their kennel name as Desamee, and Desamee Leon Hubert and

Ch Desamee Tripot de Vasouy, a French import who became a champion in the UK.

Desamee Mitzi Moffat (Maudie) were gracing the show ring. The first show that had classes for the Briard was in 1970, but things moved quickly and by 1974 there were classes at Crufts with Challenge Certificates (CCs) available. Winning three of these CCs gains a dog the title of Champion in Britain, and the first Briard to do this was Maudie herself. Sadly, she died later in 1974 after a caesarean operation. The winner of the Challenge Certificate for best dog that year at Crufts was a fawn French import, Desamee Tripot de Vasouy, who had to wait until Crufts in 1976 to win his champion title. CCs were only on offer at six shows each year at that time, but by 2000 there would be 21 pairs of CCs awarded.

Characteristics of the
BRIARD

IS THE BRIARD FOR YOU?

It is a big step to decide on a Briard as a pet, as he is large and, if not kept under control, can be exceptionally boisterous. Indeed, the main reason that Briards are given up to breed rescue services by their owners is that they are out of control. This is not in an aggressive way, but in an over-enthusiastic, bouncing and destroying-the-house sort of a way. They are too large to let run wild.

A Briard also needs some work on his coat if it is to remain beautiful. Also keep in mind that a Briard is a large dog to handle in the bath and can make the house very wet when he jumps out of the tub to avoid the towels.

Because their initial function was the guarding and droving of sheep, Briards make very good guards of the family and home. They get on very well with the family children, but are less sociable with strangers. Briards can try to dominate other dogs they meet, and at times may even challenge familiar people to see if they can become the pack leaders of their homes.

A dog like a Greyhound is very lazy inside the house, but a whirlwind of activity out of doors. Not so with the Briard—he is a whirlwind everywhere, and his big mud-encrusted feet have caused the demise of many a light-coloured fabric.

Training is absolutely vital for the Briard, and training experts consider the breed to be a little slow on the uptake when compared to German Shepherd Dogs or Border Collies. Maybe this is because the Briard had to do *some* thinking while protecting its livestock, but not as much problem-solving as the Border Collie, which performs quite complex tasks in moving its sheep. Regardless, training the Briard has to start early and continue at a steady pace.

ORIGINAL PURPOSE

To understand any breed of dog, you have to think about the job for which they were bred. Briards and the other French sheepdogs were developed for a type of sheep farming called transhumance. This means moving the sheep long distances from winter to summer pastures, and the moving flocks may have consisted of thousands of sheep. Work like this requires a dog with a bit of independent thinking.

HEALTH CONSIDERATIONS

One of the benefits of breeding in small numbers is that health considerations have an higher profile. How many health problems that are documented for the Briard will depend on what source you consult. Some lists include every illness that might have been seen in the breed and do not really give an idea of how common each one is. The health problems that I will discuss later in the health chapter of this book

CORRECTIVE SURGERY
Surgery is often used to correct genetic bone diseases in dogs. Usually the problems present themselves early in the dog's life and must be treated before bone growth stops.

are bloat or gastric torsion, which is found in all breeds with a large, deep chest; hip dysplasia, which seems to be found in all large breeds; and retinal pigment epithelial dystrophy and stationary night blindness, which are eye diseases.

The Kennel Club and the British Veterinary Association run schemes to screen all breeds for hip dysplasia and all forms of eye disease. When obtaining a puppy, make sure that your pet's parents are clear of any eye disease and that the x-rays of their hips were

as good or better than the average for Briards. Bloat is a dreadful condition, and much research is taking place on this problem that can kill an otherwise healthy dog in a matter of hours.

COLOURS

It may seem that the Briard is found only in black or fawn, with a strange bit in the standard mentioning that greys are found as well. However, the situation is actually much more complicated than this, and the only way to simplify the matter of colour is to look at Briard colour genetics. Honestly, it is the genetics that make the true colour situation easier to understand. I do realise that the most difficult part of discussing the topic of Briard colour genetics is to convince the reader not to skip over this part of the chapter! Although the word 'genetics' has an aura about it that says 'this bit is only for brain surgeons and nuclear physicists,' that is just not the case.

The key to Briard colour genetics is that two dogs that are the same colour may have ended up this way despite having different genes. Any Briard inherits half of its genetic make-up from its sire and half from its dam. The genetic material is inherited as little lumps of chemical called genes.

I find that the best analogy for genes is to consider each gene as a

Fawn is the mostly commonly seen colour in the Briard, though blacks are also seen, as well as the rarer grey coloration.

DO YOU KNOW ABOUT HIP DYSPLASIA?

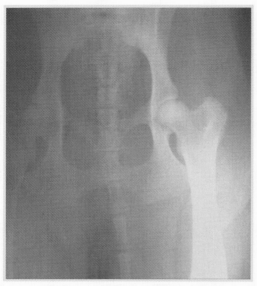

X-ray of a dog with 'Good' hips.

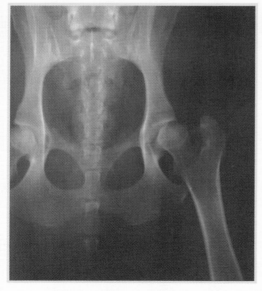

X-ray of a dog with 'Moderate' dysplastic hips.

Hip dysplasia is a fairly common condition found in pure-bred dogs. When a dog has hip dysplasia, its hind leg has an incorrectly formed hip joint. By constant use of the hip joint, it becomes more and more loose, wears abnormally and may become arthritic.

Hip dysplasia can only be confirmed with an x-ray, but certain symptoms may indicate a problem. Your dog may have an hip dysplasia problem if it walks in a peculiar manner, hops instead of smoothly runs, uses its hind legs in unison (to keep the pressure off the weak joint), has trouble getting up from a prone position or always sits with both legs together on one side of its body.

As the dog matures, it may adapt well to life with a bad hip, but in a few years the arthritis develops and many dogs with hip dysplasia become cripples.

Hip dysplasia is considered an inherited disease and only can be diagnosed definitively when the dog is two years old. Some experts claim that a special diet might help your puppy outgrow the bad hip, but the usual treatments are surgical. The removal of the pectineus muscle, the removal of the round part of the femur, reconstructing the pelvis and replacing the hip with an artificial one are all surgical interventions that are expensive, but they are usually very successful. Follow the advice of your veterinary surgeon.

book that can be borrowed from the library. Each gene is a book, a separate entity, but it also belongs to a group of books on a similar subject. Each pile of books, such as the pile of cookery books or the pile of westerns, is the equivalent of what is called a gene series. The gene series can contain many different genes; a series can be large, like the huge pile of cookery books, or it may be very small, like the number of books written on photographing goldfish.

The rules of this library are that the borrower has to take one book from each pile as a present from mother, and another from each pile as a present from father, in the same way that a gene from each series is inherited by the Briard from sire and dam.

To make things more interesting, the borrower can take a copy of the same book from father and from mother. For the Briard, this would be inheriting the same gene from both its sire and dam. In this case, the dog is said to be homozygous for this gene (homo, meaning 'same' and zygous, meaning 'new individual').

The borrower could take two different books from the pile. In this case, for the Briard, it would be inheriting two different genes from the same series, one from each parent. For this gene, the dog would be called heterozygous, from hetero, meaning 'different.'

THE B OR BLACK SERIES

The first category is the B or black series. The gene b is rarely present in the Briard: most are BB. The gene B must be present for black pigment to be made. When B is present, we see the colour black in the Briard. This gene is expressed as black nose, black lips, black eyelids and any black in the coat.

Illustrated Briard with at least one gene that is B.

Illustrated Briard that would have to be bb.

The gene B covers the presence of the gene b. In genetic terms, B is dominant to b; b is recessive to B.

A Briard that happened to be Bb would be indistinguishable from the BB dog in appearance, because B is the dominant gene. The Bb dog would still have a black nose, black lips and black eyelids. However, a Briard that was bb would be incapable of making the colour black. Anywhere that should have been black would be liver or chocolate, so it would have a liver nose, lips and eyelids.

Liver-coloured Pointers and chocolate Labradors have this bb conformation. Liver-coloured dogs cannot have black noses.

THE D OR DILUTION SERIES

The next category is the D or dilution series. There are just two genes in this series: D, which is dominant to d; and d, which is

INTUITIVE BEHAVIOUR

Though the Briard can be boisterous, if there are old, infirm or very young children about they behave in a much more gentle way. Briards have been kind and affectionate visitors to old people's homes, and they have been seen to communicate with autistic children in a way that no human could.

recessive to D. If a Briard has the gene D, the pigment will be seen at its full intensity; in other words, black will be black. The Dd dog will be indistinguishable in appearance from the DD dog because the D is dominant.

A Briard that is dd has the pigment in each hair reduced. There is not full colour, but dilute colour. Black appears as blue, and liver appears as yellow. As liver is not found in the Briard, its dilute form is not found either. The blue

Illustrated Briard with at least one gene that is D.

Illustrated Briard that would have to be dd.

dog cannot have a black nose, so its nose, lips and eyelids are blue.

There are two types of black Briard, the homozygous form (DD) and the heterozygous form (Dd). There is only one form of blue dog, dd. When geneticists try to predict what might result from a mating, they write out the genes available in a square. If a DD dog was mated to a dd dog, we would have:

Homozygous blue (dd)

		d	d
Homozygous black (DD)	D	Dd	Dd
	D	Dd	Dd

This mating gives only one colour, heterozygous black. All these puppies appear black just like their black parent, but if two of them were mated together we would have a 25% chance of breeding a blue, as shown in the following square:

Heterozygous black (Dd)

		D	d
Heterozygous black (Dd)	D	DD	Dd
	d	Dd	dd

SOME PET FACTS
- 94% of pet owners keep a pet's photo on display in their home or office.
- 46% of pets sleep on their owners' beds.
- 63% of us celebrate our pets' birthdays.
- 66% of us take our pets to the vet more often than we see our own physicians!

This brings us to the problem of population genetics. The very first genetic experiments were done by an Austrian monk called Gregor Mendel, who used pea plants. He carried out thousands of pea matings before publishing his original paper in 1865, which was shamefully disregarded during his lifetime. It was only because he had worked with so many pea plants that his calculations worked out exactly. Since Briard litters *(thankfully)* do not contain hundreds of puppies, we do not get perfect ratios. We cannot predict the number of puppies of each colour born, but we can predict which colours are possible.

Therefore, when two heterozygous blacks are mated together, all that we can say for certain is that the mating could produce homozygous black, heterozygous black and homozygous blue puppies. The two types of black appear exactly the same in colour, and probably there will not be many blues.

A: Dominant black, the puppy is born black and stays black.

a^y: Dominant yellow, the puppy is born sable, but this fades to leave fawn on the adult dog.

THE A OR AGOUTI SERIES

This gene series is named after a South American rodent called an agouti, which looks a little like a giant guinea pig. Agoutis are a sable-type colour, and this series of genes includes the colour sable.

The standard textbook description of this gene series gives five genes, but I think that it is more complex than this, especially in the case of the Briard. The usual five are:

A: dominant black—the puppy is born black and stays

completely black;

a^y: dominant yellow—the puppy is born sable but at adulthood the black has faded, leaving the coat completely yellow;

a^g: the puppy is born sable and remains sable;

a^s: the puppy is born with a saddle of black with extensive yellow and remains like this;

a^t: the puppy is born black and tan like a Beauceron and remains like this.

There must be at least one other gene in this series, one which the Airedale Terrier has,

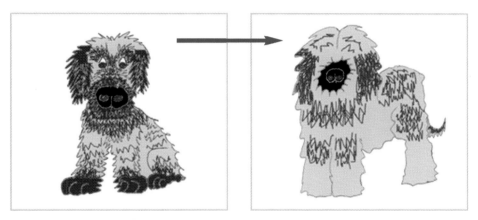

a^g: The puppy is born sable and remains sable as an adult.

a^s: The puppy is born with a black saddle and grows up like this.

a^t: The puppy is born black and tan (like a Beauceron) and remains like this.

a^a: The puppy is born black and tan but develops a saddle as an adult dog (like an Airedale Terrier).

which causes the puppy to be born with coloration like that of a Beauceron, but the colour changes to just a saddle of dark colour. Perhaps we should name this gene a^a: the puppy is born the black and tan of a Beauceron and fades in colour to the black and tan of an adult Airedale Terrier. To work out where this comes in as far as being dominant/recessive, we would need data from matings of dogs of this colour.

However, we do not want all of these genes in the Briard. We

have A, a^y, a^g and a tiny remnant population of a^t that everyone has been trying to eradicate for over 100 years. It does not seem that a^s and a^a are present in the breed.

With so many genes for sable available, and the possibility of them 'mixing and matching' together (heterozygous arrangements), no wonder there are so many different shades of fawn in the Briard.

THE E OR EXTENSION OF BLACK INTO THE COAT SERIES

There are two genes in this series that affect the Briard:

E^m: having a black mask (and ears);
E: not having a black mask.

Most fawn Briards have the black points. It is not possible to see if a black has a black mask.

The black and tan of the Airedale puppy differs from the black and tan coloration of the Beauceron.

E: Not having a mask

E^m : Having a black mask.

TAKING CARE

Science is showing that as people take care of their pets, the pets are taking care of their owners. A study in 1998, published in the *American Journal of Cardiology,* found that having a pet can prolong his owner's life. Pet owners generally have lower blood pressure, and pets help their owners to relax and keep more physically fit. It was also found that pets help to keep the elderly connected to their communities..

The G or Greying Series

Just as with all of the subtle sable fawns, there is a gene series that affects the intensity of the colour of black. The gene G causes greying of the coat—not the gradual greying of age, but the greying that is found in breeds like the Bedlington Terrier in which the coat progressively changes in colour until it has become a blue shade. However, the nose, eyelids and lips remain black.

The two genes in this series are G, giving greying, which is dominant to g, in which the colour remains the same and does not go grey.

The two genes give three combinations:

GG: born black, coat fades to grey/blue, nose remains black;
Gg: born black, coat fades to grey/blue, nose remains black;
gg: born black, stays black.

The Blue Problem

We have given the different ways that a Briard can be blue, either by the dilution gene d or by the greying gene G. Some describe the

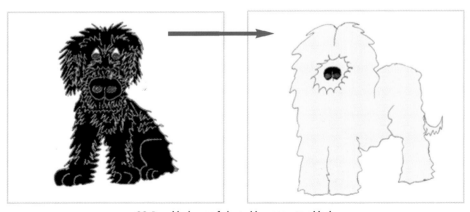

GG: Born black, coat fades to blue, nose stays black.

BIG HEART

The French actress Gaby Morley described the Briard as a 'big heart wrapped up in fur,' a quote that many Briard lovers feel sums up the breed.

d blue as 'blue born blue,' and the G blue as 'blue born black.' The problem with the d blue is that it cannot have a black nose, which is against the edicts of the standard. Perhaps it is time for the senior breeders of the world to consider the genetic impossibility of a dog of a recognised colour having a black nose.

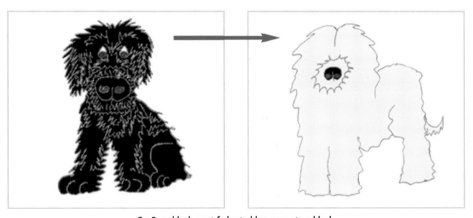

Gg: Born black, coat fades to blue, nose stays black.

gg: Born black, and remains black as an adult.

As for the G for greying with the fawns, this just adds to the possibilities of a myriad of shades.

The British breed standard gives the acceptable colours as 'All black, or with white hairs scattered throughout the black coat. Fawn in all its shades, darker shades preferred. Fawns may have dark shadings on ears, muzzle, back and tail, but these shadings must blend gradually into the rest of the coat since any

DO YOU WANT TO LIVE LONGER?

If you like to volunteer, it is wonderful if you can take your dog to a nursing home once a week for several hours. The elder community loves to have a dog with which to visit, and often your dog will bring a bit of companionship to someone who is lonely or somewhat detached from the world. You will be not only bringing happiness to someone else but also keeping your dog busy—and we haven't even mentioned the fact that it has been discovered that volunteering helps to increase your own longevity!

DOGS, DOGS, GOOD FOR YOUR HEART!

People usually purchase dogs for companionship, but studies show that dogs can help to improve their owners' health and level of activity, as well as lower a human's risk of coronary heart disease. Without even realising it, when a person puts time into exercising, grooming and feeding a dog, he also puts more time into his own personal health care. Dog owners establish more routine schedules for their dogs to follow, which can have positive effects on a human's health. Dogs also teach us patience, offer unconditional love and provide the joy of having a furry friend to pet!

demarcation line denotes a bicolour which is not permissible. May also be slate grey.'

As we can see, the situation is a little more complex than these few lines indicate.

The blue Briard has a blue nose due to the presence of the dilution gene dd.

Breed Standard for the
BRIARD

Breed standards were devised in Britain during the Victorian era, after the development of the dog show. Dog shows spread to France in 1863, just four years after the first recorded show was held in Britain, in Newcastle. The first Briard standard was drawn up by the members of the Club Français du Chien du Berger (French Club

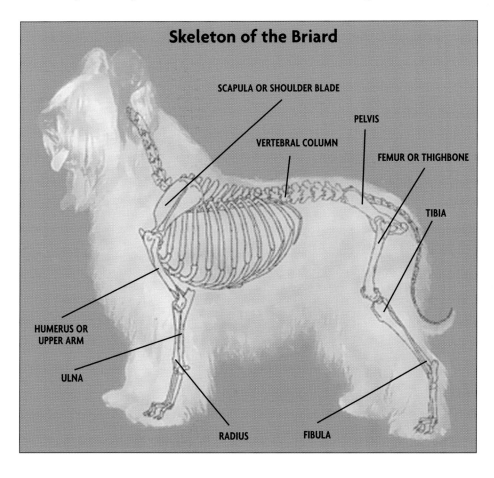

Skeleton of the Briard

SCAPULA OR SHOULDER BLADE

PELVIS

VERTEBRAL COLUMN

FEMUR OR THIGHBONE

TIBIA

HUMERUS OR
UPPER ARM

ULNA

RADIUS

FIBULA

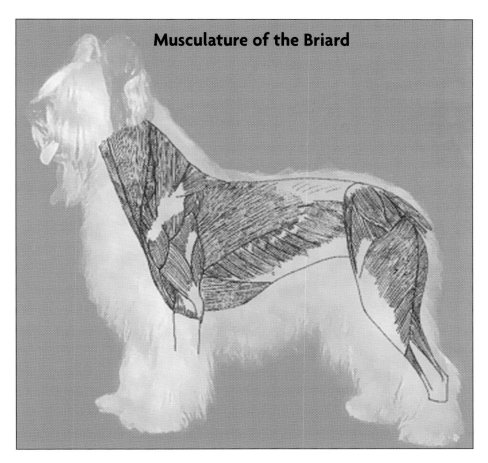

Musculature of the Briard

for Sheepdogs) in 1897. The President of this club was Monsieur Boulet, a gentleman who was interested in gundogs as well as sheepdogs, and who created the breed named after him, the Boulet Griffon, which can be considered as a sort of French wire-haired pointer.

The breeding and showing of pedigreed dogs was an activity mainly carried out by those with a sufficient amount of money to have a substantial amount of leisure time. At that time, people also had a better knowledge of animal construction than we have today, because the principal modes of transport during their lifetimes had involved horses. If the horse was not correctly constructed, then the chances were that the people would not get where they were going.

Any description that uses just words is open to many interpretations, and we have to work harder to envision what the breed standard means because we start with a lot less 'instinctive' knowledge than those who first wrote the standard.

The standard in use in Britain is a very close translation of the French standard as revised there in 1911. The Kennel Club revised it in 1977, with few changes except a small change in the minimum size.

The most outstanding dogs will win under all judges; opinions tend to differ when it comes to the faulty dogs. The all-

rounder judge will tend to give first place to the dog with the best conformation, while the breed specialist would have problems giving a prize to this dog if its tail did not have the characteristic hooked tip or if there was something wrong with the double dewclaws, two of the special features of the breed.

THE KENNEL CLUB STANDARD FOR THE BRIARD

General Appearance: Rugged appearance; supple, muscular and well proportioned.

Characteristics: Very intelligent, gay and lively.

Temperament: Fearless, with no trace of timidity or aggressiveness.

Head and Skull: Skull slightly

THE IDEAL SPECIMEN

According to The Kennel Club, 'The Breed Standard is the "Blueprint" of the ideal specimen in each breed approved by a governing body, e.g. The Kennel Club, the Fédération Cynologique Internationale (FCI) and the American Kennel Club.

'The Kennel Club writes and revises Breed Standards taking account of the advice of Breed Councils/Clubs. Breed Standards are not changed lightly to avoid "changing the standard to fit the current dogs" and the health and well-being of future dogs is always taken into account when new standards are prepared or existing ones altered.'

Briards entered in dog shows are compared to the breed standard. The Briard that mostly closely conforms to the standard, in the judge's opinion, is selected as Best of Breed.

rounded and slightly longer from occiput to stop than it is wide when measured through points of cheekbones. Head is composed of two equal rectangles, occiput to stop and stop to end of nose, when viewed in profile from above. Muzzle square and very strong; any tendency to snipiness highly undesirable. Stop clearly defined. Nose large and square, always black.

Eyes: Horizontally placed, well open and rather large, not oblique.

Intelligent and gentle in expression. Dark brown, eye rims always black.

Ears: Set on high and covered with long hair. Should not lie too flat against side of head. Fairly short, length of ear being equal to or slightly less than half length of head. When dog alert ears should be lifted slightly and swing slightly forward.

Mouth: Teeth very strong and white with a perfect, regular and

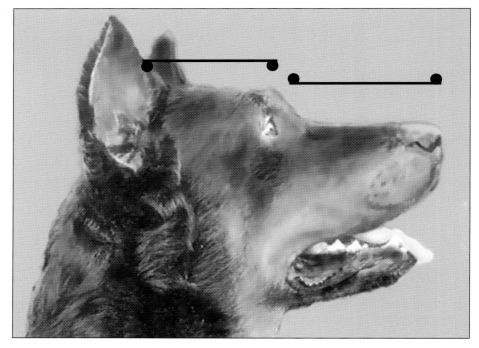

complete scissor bite, i.e. upper teeth closely overlapping lower teeth and set square to the jaws. Lips always black.

Neck: Of good length; strong and muscular; arched, giving proud carriage of head and flowing smoothly into well placed shoulders.

Forequarters: Shoulders well angulated and well laid back, forelegs well muscled, strongly boned.

Body: Back firm and level, chest broad, medium spring of rib, well let down, very slight slope at croup, determining set of tail. Very slightly longer in body than height at shoulder.

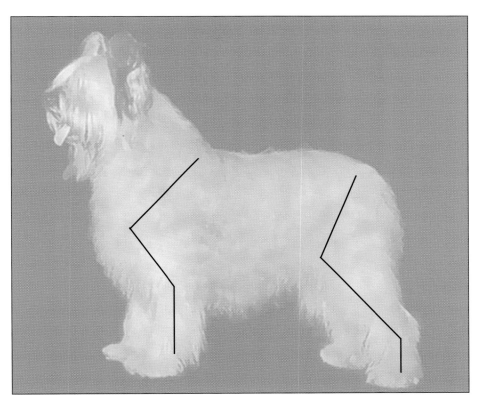

Correct angulation in the Briard.

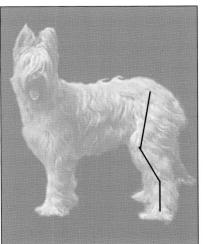
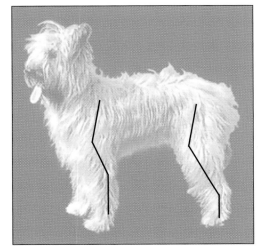

The dog on the left has poor hind angulation. He would walk the same way you would if you did not bend your knees, and there is no way he could perform his daily duties as an herder with this construction. The dog on the right has equally poor angulation in both the fore- and hind-quarters.

BRIARD

A Briard wins a Group placement at an FCI show on the Continent.

The Briard's gait should be effortless and strong with plenty of drive. Exhibitors must move their dogs in the show ring to demonstrate that the dogs possess the desired gait.

Hindquarters: Well angulated, with hocks set not too low and turning neither in nor out, but leg below hock not quite vertical. Hindlegs, particularly thighs, well muscled. Double dewclaws set low on hindlegs of utmost importance.

Feet: Strong, turning neither in nor out, slightly rounded, about midway between cat foot and hare foot. Nails always black, pads firm and hard, toes close together. Well covered with hair.

Tail: Long, well covered with hair with upward hook at tip. Carried low but always held centrally. Bone of tail reaching at least point of hock.

Gait/Movement: Effortless, and when dog extends himself covering a great deal of ground. Extremely supple, enabling dog to turn quickly. Strong, firm, very smooth with plenty of drive.

Coat: Long, not less than 7 cms (3 ins) on body. Slightly wavy and very dry. A fine dense undercoat required all over body. Head carries hair forming a moustache, beard and eyebrows, lightly veiling eyes.

Colour: All black, or with white hairs scattered through black coat. Fawn in all its shades, darker shades preferred. Fawns may have dark shadings on ears, muzzle, back and tail, but these shadings

Four Briards, two with cropped ears and two with natural drop ears. All are good, sound examples of the breed. Note the good hooked tail on the cropped black dog. The balance of the uncropped fawn dog has been a little lost because the dog is slightly too outstretched.

must blend gradually into rest of coat since any demarcation line denotes a bicolour which is not permissible. May also be slate grey.

Size: Height: dogs 62–68 cms (24.5–27 ins) at withers; bitches: 56–64 cms (22–25.5 ins) at withers. Slight undersize before 18 months, or slight oversize in maturity permissible.

Faults: Any departure from the foregoing points should be considered a fault and the seriousness with which the fault should be regarded should be in exact proportion to its degree.

Note: Male animals should have two apparently normal testicles fully descended into the scrotum.

COMMENTS ON THE STANDARD

As with any breed standard, it would not be possible to read it to a particularly artistic person with no knowledge of dogs and have them draw a Briard. I'm not sure that he would be able to manage to draw something even resembling a dog. This is because those who drew up the standard were so immersed in livestock that they had a large amount of implicit knowledge, information that was so much a part of them that they did not realise that future generations would not

Correct topline on the Briard. A firm, level back has the strongest muscles to help the Briard work all day.

Roached topline (computer-generated fault).

Dippy topline (computer-generated fault).

This tail is incorrect for a Briard as it has no hook on the end.

This is a Briard with a correct tail, but note that the toes on its left hind foot are pointing straight at you instead of straight ahead.

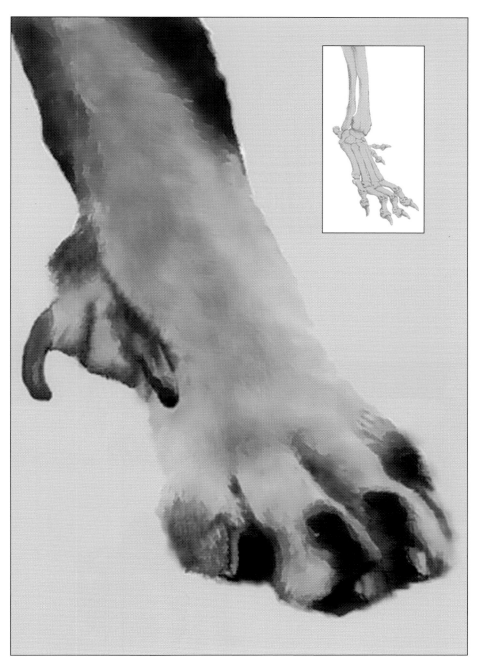

The double dewclaw on the back legs of a Beauceron. The Briard has this same structure. The inset shows the skeletal appearance of the double dewclaw. The two dewclaws are made of three bones each, with the nail at the end.

DEWCLAWS IN FRANCE

In France, there are very strict rules about the structure of the dewclaws, as not every Briard has them as fully formed as in the ideal structure illustrated here. It is permissible to have the bones of the two toes fused together, and it is permissible to have the two proximal phalanges missing (giving 'floating dew-claws'). If two phalanges are missing from one dewclaw, it is not permissible for the dog to be awarded the CAC, the certificate necessary for the title of French Champion. If four phalanges are missing, the dog would be disqualified in France.

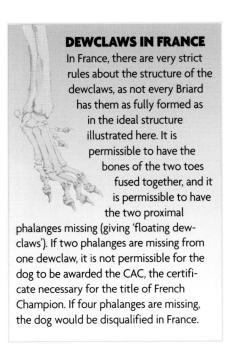

instinctively know what they meant.

The whole object of a breed standard is to describe a dog that has both perfect conformation and breed points. What is perfect conformation? It means that all of the bones are correctly formed and join together at the joints at the correct angles so they can flex and move in the most efficient way. This results in a dog that seems to move with no effort, a dog that could run after sheep from dawn to dusk.

What are breed points? These are the features that say 'I am a Briard.' All dogs should have perfect conformation, but only a

Briard has the combination of the hook at the end of its tail, the double dewclaws and a head formed from rectangles that are covered with Briard-quality hair in a Briard way.

It is not as easy to see the structure of the head of the Briard as it is to see the structure of the head of a breed such as a Borzoi because of the Briard's profuse coat. The way to find out what really is going on under all that hair is to gently feel the proportions. The stop (the indentation at the eyes) should be halfway from the back of the skull (the occiput) to the nose. The standard describes very well the rectangles that form the head, and if we look at pictures of what is effectively the smooth-haired Briard, the Beauceron, we can see them. The heads of both the Briard and the Beauceron demonstrate horizontally placed eyes and a large nose. From the front, the muzzle forms a smaller rectangle within the larger square of the whole head.

SNIPEY

A snipe is a game bird that would have often been seen on the dinner tables of 19th-century aristocracy. It has a long pointed nose; thus the term 'snipiness' refers to a muzzle with a lack of strength in the underjaw. The Briard has a strong jaw to go with its big strong white teeth.

Eye colour affects the expression. The dark eye, as required by the standard, gives a much kinder expression. The Briard's eye on the right has been altered by computer to appear light.

The head of the Beauceron demonstrates the horizontally placed eyes, as in the Briard as well, and the large nose. From the front, the muzzle forms a smaller rectangle within the large square of the head.

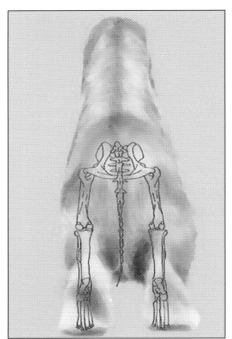

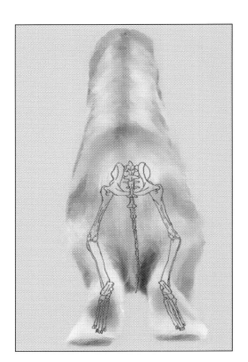

Rear view of the Briard (computer-generated illustration). The dog on the upper left has correct hindlegs; the whole assembly is more or less parallel. The dog on the upper right demonstrates cowhocks, where the bones forming the hocks veer towards each other. The dog below has bow hocks, the joints being widely separated from each other.

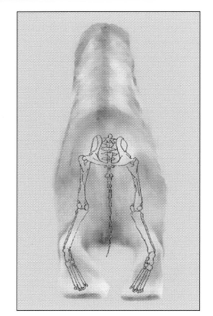

Eye colour affects the Briard's expression. The dark eye, as required by the standard, gives a much kinder expression than a light eye. The Briard should possess a correct scissor bite, in which the upper teeth closely overlap the lower ones, giving an efficient cutting bite.

In Britain, the ears of the Briard are not cropped, so lie at the sides of the head. They are very mobile ears, expressing the dog's emotion.

Wide front.

Narrow front.

Correct front.

The natural drop ears of the Briard are expressive and mobile.

BRIARD

If you are absolutely sure that the Briard is the breed for you, then it is important to realise the amount of work that goes into making a member of this breed physically

PUPPY SELECTION

Your selection of a good puppy can be determined by your needs. A show potential or a good pet? It is your choice. Every puppy, however, should be of good temperament. Although show-quality puppies are bred and raised with emphasis on physical conformation, responsible breeders strive for equally good temperament. Do not buy from a breeder who concentrates solely on physical beauty at the expense of personality.

and mentally presentable to the rest of the world.

As with all larger breeds, the growth curve is from puppy until the age of eighteen months (adult), from adult until the age of seven or eight years and from then on, a senior dog. Every day after the age of eleven is an extra blessing.

It is possible to obedience-train your Briard to a high standard, but it will be harder than going through the same training programme with a breed like the Border Collie. A Briard gets bored if asked to perform the same task repeatedly, and will often refuse after doing something three or four times.

All dogs like consistency, so you must use the same commands for the same requested behaviour. For example, the word 'down' should have a specific meaning to your puppy and should be used in the same way by all household members. In other words, 'down' should not mean 'lie on the ground' when you say it, 'stop jumping up' when the children say it and 'get off the sofa' when granny says it. If one word is used for all of these things, not only will your puppy not understand but he also will be utterly confused. Your Briard will want to please you, so you will need to demonstrate clearly and consistently to your puppy what behaviour is acceptable.

In the beginning, there will be a period of settling in, and you must be prepared for some mishaps around the home during the first few weeks of your life together. It will be important that your precious ornaments are kept well out of harm's (meaning the puppy's) way, and you will have to think twice about where you place hot cups of coffee or anything breakable. Accidents can and do happen, so you will need to think ahead so as to avoid them. Electric cables must be carefully concealed, and your puppy must be taught where he can go and where he cannot go.

Before making your commitment to a new puppy, do also think carefully about you future holiday plans. Depending on the country in which you live, your dog may or may not be able to travel abroad with you. If you have thought things through carefully and discussed the matter thoroughly with all members of your family, hopefully you will have come to the right decision. If you decide that a Briard should join your family, this will hopefully be a happy, long-term relationship for all parties concerned.

PREPARING FOR PUP

Unfortunately, when a puppy is bought by someone who does not take into consideration the time and attention that dog ownership requires, it is the puppy who suffers when he is either abandoned or placed in a shelter by a frustrated owner. So all of the 'homework' you do in preparation for your pup's arrival will benefit you both. The more informed you are, the more you will know what to expect and the better equipped you will be to handle the ups and downs of raising a puppy. Hopefully, everyone in the household is willing to do his part in raising and caring for the pup. The anticipation of owning a dog often brings a lot of promises from excited family members: 'I will walk him every day,' 'I will feed him,' 'I will house-train him,' etc., but these things take time and effort, and promises can easily be forgotten once the novelty of the new pet has worn off.

BUYING A BRIARD PUPPY

Although you may be looking for a Briard as a pet dog rather than as a show dog, this does not mean that you want a dog that is in any way 'second-rate.' A caring breeder will have brought up the entire litter of puppies with the same amount of dedication, and a puppy destined for a pet home should be just as healthy as one that hopes to end up in the show ring.

Because you have carefully selected this breed, you will want a Briard that is a typical specimen, both in looks and in temperament. In your endeavours to find such a puppy, you will have to select the breeder with care. The Kennel Club will almost certainly be able to give you names of contacts within the Briard breed clubs. These people can possibly put you in touch with breeders who may have puppies for sale. However, although they can point you in the right direction, it will be up to you to do your homework carefully.

Even though you are probably not looking for a show dog, it is always a good idea to visit a larger show so that you may see quality specimens of the breed. This will also give you an opportunity to meet breeders who should be able to answer some of your queries. In addition, you will get some idea about which breeders appear to take most care of their stock and are likely to have given their puppies the best possible start in life. Something else you may be able to decide upon is which colour appeals to you most, although this is purely personal preference.

When buying your puppy, you will need to know about vaccinations: which ones have been given already and which ones the puppy still needs. It is important that any injections already given by a veterinary surgeon have been recorded and documented for proof. A worming routine is also vital for any young puppy, so the breeder should be able to tell you exactly what treatment has been given, when it was administered and how you should continue.

Clearly, when selecting a puppy, the one you must choose must be in good condition. The coat should look healthy and there should be no discharge from the eyes or nose. Ears should also be clean and, of course, there should be absolutely no signs of parasites. Check that the skin is healthy and free of rashes and any other irritations. Of course, the puppy you choose should not have any evidence of loose stool.

As in several other breeds, some Briard puppies have umbilical hernias, which can be seen as a small lump on the tummy where the umbilical cord was attached. It is preferable not

Never select a Briard that is any way 'second-rate.' Even if your chosen family dog will never see a show ring, you still want to buy a sound, friendly and typical representative of this great French breed.

to have such an hernia on any puppy, and you should check for this at the outset. If an hernia is present, you should discuss its seriousness with the breeder. Most umbilical hernias are safe, but your vet should keep an eye on it in case an operation is needed.

Just a few words of warning: be very careful about where you purchase your puppy. Find your breeder through a reputable source, like a breed club, and visit the quarters in which the puppies are kept. Always insist that you see the puppy's dam and, if possible, the sire. Frequently the

sire will not be owned by the litter's breeder, but a photograph may be available for you to see. Ask if the breeder has any other of the puppy's relatives that you can meet. For example, there may be an older half-sister or half-brother on the premises, and it would be interesting for you to see how the relative has turned out: its eventual size, coat quality, temperament and so on.

Be sure, too, that if you decide to buy a puppy, all relevant documentation is provided at the time of sale. You will need a copy of the pedigree, preferably Kennel

Club registration documents, vaccination certificates and a feeding chart so that you know exactly how the puppy has been fed and how you should continue. Some careful breeders provide their puppy buyers with a small amount of food. This prevents the risk of an upset tummy, allowing for a gradual change of diet if that particular brand of food is not locally available.

COMMITMENT OF OWNERSHIP

After considering all of these factors, you have already made some very important decisions about selecting your puppy. You have chosen a Briard, which means that you have decided which characteristics you want in a dog and what type of dog will best fit into your family and lifestyle. If you have selected a breeder, you have gone a step further—you have done your research and found a responsible, conscientious person who breeds

INSURANCE
Many good breeders will offer you insurance with your new puppy, which is an excellent idea. The first few weeks of insurance will probably be covered free of charge or with only minimal cost, allowing you to take up the policy when this expires. If you own a pet dog, it is sensible to take out such a policy as veterinary fees can be high, although routine vaccinations and boosters are not covered. Look carefully at the many options open to you before deciding which suits you best.

quality Briards and who should be a reliable source of help as you and your puppy adjust to life together. If you have observed a litter in action, you have obtained a firsthand look at the dynamics of a puppy 'pack' and, thus, you should learn about each pup's individual personality—perhaps you have even found one that particularly appeals to you.

However, even if you have not yet found the Briard puppy of your dreams, observing pups will help you learn to recognise certain behaviour and to determine what a pup's behaviour indicates about his temperament. You will be able to pick out which pups are leaders, which ones are less outgoing, which ones are confident, which ones

A well-bred and obedience-trained Briard can make a dependable, biddable home companion and guard.

are shy, playful, friendly, aggressive, etc. Equally as important, you will learn to recognise what an healthy pup should look and act like. All of these things will help you in your search, and when you find the Briard that was meant for you, you will know it!

DOCUMENTATION

Two important documents you will get from the breeder are the pup's pedigree and registration certificate. The breeder should register the litter and each pup individually with The Kennel Club, and it is necessary for you to have the paperwork if you plan on showing or breeding in the future.

Make sure you know the breeder's intentions on which type of registration he will obtain for the pup. There are limited registrations that may prohibit the dog from being shown, bred or competing in non-conformation trials such as Working or Agility if the breeder feels that the pup is not of sufficient quality to do so. There is also a type of registration that will permit the dog in non-conformation competition only.

On the reverse side of the registration certificate, the new owner can find the transfer section, which must be signed by the breeder.

GETTING ACQUAINTED

You should not even think about buying a puppy that looks sick, undernourished, overly frightened or nervous. Sometimes a timid puppy will warm up to you after a 30-minute 'let's-get-acquainted' session.

Researching your breed, selecting a responsible breeder and observing as many pups as possible are all important steps on the way to dog ownership. It may seem like a lot of effort… and you have not even brought the pup home yet! Remember, though, you cannot be too careful when it comes to deciding on the type of dog you want and finding about your prospective pup's background. Buying a puppy is not—nor should it be—just another whimsical purchase. This is one instance in which you actually get to choose your own family. You may be thinking that

AN ACCEPTABLE AGE

Breeders rarely release puppies until they are eight to ten weeks of age. This is an acceptable age for most breeds of dog, though breeders of the smallest and largest breeds often do not release the puppies until 12 weeks.

buying a puppy should be fun—it should not be so serious and so much work. Keep in mind that your puppy is not a cuddly stuffed toy or decorative lawn ornament, but a creature that will become a real member of your family. You will come to realise that, while buying a puppy is a pleasurable and exciting endeavour, it is not something to be taken lightly. Relax…the fun will start when the pup comes home!

Always keep in mind that a puppy is nothing more than a baby in furry disguise…a baby who is virtually helpless in a human world and who trusts his owner for fulfilment of his basic needs for survival. In addition to water and shelter, your pup needs care, protection, guidance and love. If you are not prepared to commit to this, then you are not prepared to own a dog.

Wait a minute, you say. How hard could this be? All of my neighbours own dogs and they seem to be doing just fine. Why should I have to worry about all of this? Well, you should not worry about it; in fact you will probably find that once your Briard pup gets used to his new home, he will fall into his place in the family quite naturally. But it never hurts to emphasise the commitment of dog ownership. With some time and patience, it is really not excessively difficult to raise a curious and exuberant Briard pup to be a well-adjusted and well-mannered adult dog—a dog that could be your most loyal friend.

PREPARING PUPPY'S PLACE IN YOUR HOME

Researching your breed and finding a breeder are only two aspects of the 'homework' you will have to do before bringing your Briard puppy home. You will also have to prepare your home and family for the new addition. Much as you would prepare a nursery for a newborn baby, you will need to designate a place in your home that will be the puppy's home. How you prepare your home will depend on how much freedom the dog will be allowed. Whatever you decide, you must ensure that he has a place that he can 'call his own.'

When you bring your new puppy into your home, you are bringing him into what will be his home as well. Obviously, you did not buy a puppy so that he could

BOY OR GIRL?
The sex of your puppy is an important consideration to be discussed. A bitch may be better as a family companion as she is generally more tolerant and will be less dominant and physically strong than an adult male.

take over your house, but in order for a puppy to grow into a stable, well-adjusted dog, he has to feel comfortable in his surroundings. Remember, he is leaving the warmth and security of his mother and littermates, as well as the familiarity of the only place he has ever known, so it is important to make his transition as easy as possible. By preparing a place in your home for the puppy you are making him feel as welcome as possible in a strange new place. It should not take him long to get used to it, but the sudden shock of being transplanted is somewhat traumatic for a young pup. Imagine how a small child would

ARE YOU A FIT OWNER?
If the breeder from whom you are buying a puppy asks you a lot of personal questions, do not be insulted. Such a breeder wants to be sure that you will be a fit provider for his puppy.

FEEDING TIPS

You should start feeding exactly the same food that the puppy has been getting from his breeder; the breeder should give you a few days' supply as well as a diet sheet. Hopefully this will be a complete puppy diet, so do not give your puppy too many treats (helpful for coaxing, training and rewards) as this will upset the balance of this carefully constructed *complete* diet.

Veterinary bedding in the dog's bed will help the dog to feel more at home and you may also like to pop in a blanket. This will take the place of the leaves, twigs, etc., that the pup would use in the wild to make a den; the pup can make his own 'burrow' in his bed. Although your pup is far removed from his den making-ancestors, the denning instinct is still a part of his genetic make-up. Second, until you bring your pup home, he has been sleeping amid the warmth of his mother and litter-mates, and while a blanket is not the same as a warm, breathing body, it still provides heat and something with which to snuggle. You will want to wash your pup's bedding frequently in case he has an accident in his bed, and replace or remove any blanket that becomes ragged and starts to fall apart.

feel in the same situation—that is how your puppy must be feeling. It is up to you to reassure him and to let him know, 'Little *berger*, you are going to like it here!'

WHAT YOU SHOULD BUY

BED AND BEDDING
Every dog should have his own bed, a place where he can retreat from the world. For a Briard, this has to be one of the larger sizes.

YOUR SCHEDULE . . .
If you lead an erratic, unpredictable life, with daily or weekly changes in your work requirements, consider the problems of owning a puppy. The new puppy has to be fed regularly, socialised (loved, petted, handled, introduced to other people) and, most importantly, allowed to visit outdoors for toilet training. As the dog gets older, it can be more tolerant of deviations in its feeding and toilet relief.

Toys

Toys are a must for dogs of all ages, especially curious playful pups. Puppies are the 'children' of the dog world, and what child does not love toys? Chew toys provide entertainment to both dog and owner—your dog will enjoy playing with his favourite toys, while you will enjoy the fact that they distract him from your expensive shoes and leather sofa. Puppies love to chew; in fact, chewing is a physical need for pups as they are teething, and everything looks appetising! The full range of your possessions— from old tea towel to Oriental rug—are fair game in the eyes of a teething pup. Puppies are not all

TOYS, TOYS, TOYS!

There are a large variety of dog toys available, and so many that look like they would be a lot of fun for a dog, so be careful in your selection. It is amazing what a set of puppy teeth can do to an innocent-looking toy, so, obviously, safety is a major considera-tion. Be sure to choose the most durable products that you can find. Hard nylon bones and toys are a safe bet, and many of them are offered in different flavours that will be sure to capture your dog's attention. It is fun to play a game of catch with your dog, but the Briard adult can grow tired by retrieving, so balls and Frisbees may not be considered fun forever.

The Briard puppy will welcome soft furry toys for play, but always supervise the puppy whenever he has a potentially destructible toy.

that discerning when it comes to finding something to literally 'sink their teeth into'— everything tastes great!

Briard puppies grow quickly and only the hardest, strongest toys should be offered to them.

Breeders advise owners to resist stuffed toys, because they can become de-stuffed in no time. The overly excited pup may ingest the stuffing, which is neither digestible nor nutritious, and may be dangerous.

Similarly, squeaky toys are quite popular, but take great care with them. A pup may 'disembowel' one of these and the small plastic squeaker inside can be dangerous if swallowed. Monitor the condition of all your pup's toys carefully and get rid of any that have been chewed to the point of becoming potentially dangerous.

Be careful of natural bones, which have a tendency to splinter into sharp, dangerous pieces that may perforate the bowel. Also be careful of rawhide, which can turn into long stringy pieces that are easy to swallow and choke on, or into a mushy mess on your carpet.

LEAD

A nylon lead is probably the best option as it is the most resistant to puppy teeth should your pup take a liking to chewing on his lead. Of course, this is a habit that should be nipped in the bud, but if your pup likes to chew on his lead he has a very slim chance of being able to chew through the strong nylon. Nylon leads are also lightweight, which is good for a young Briard who is just getting used to the idea of walking on a lead. For everyday walking and safety purposes, the nylon lead is a good choice. Flexible leads are not a good idea for big dogs because of the lack of control. Of course, there are special thin leads for showing purposes, but these are not sturdy enough for routine walks.

COLLAR

Putting a collar on a puppy may be an upsetting experience. Gentle reassurance of the puppy and gentle perseverance on the part of the owner will soon make the puppy realise that he is quite safe.

Your pup should get used to wearing a collar all the time since you will attach his ID tags to it; plus you need to attach the lead to something. A lightweight nylon collar is a good choice; make sure that it fits snugly enough so that the pup cannot wriggle out of it, but is loose enough so that it will not be uncomfortably tight around the pup's neck. You should be able to fit a finger between the pup and the collar. It may take some time for your pup to get used to wearing the collar, but soon he will not even notice it.

FOOD AND WATER BOWLS

Your pup will need two bowls, one for food and one for water. You may want two sets of bowls, one for inside and one for outside. Stainless steel or sturdy plastic bowls are popular choices. Plastic bowls are more chewable. Dogs tend not to chew on the steel variety, which can be sterilised. It is important to buy sturdy bowls since anything is in danger of being chewed by puppy teeth and you do not want your dog to be constantly chewing apart his bowl (for his safety and for your purse).

Purchase the largest and sturdiest feeding bowls for your Briard. These will available wherever you purchase pet supplies.

Your local pet shop sells an array of dishes and bowls for water and food. Stands to elevate the bowls are also recommended; this is a way to prevent bloat.

CLEANING SUPPLIES

Until a pup is house-trained, you will be doing a lot of cleaning. 'Accidents' will occur, which is okay in the beginning because the puppy does not know any better. All you can do is be prepared to clean up any accidents. Old rags, towels, newspapers and a safe disinfectant are good to have on hand.

BEYOND THE BASICS

The items previously discussed are the bare necessities. You will find out what else you need as you go along—grooming supplies, flea/tick protection, baby gates to partition a room, etc. These things will vary depending on your situation, but it is important that you will have everything you need to feed and make your Briard comfortable in his first few days at home.

A Briard puppy will follow his nose everywhere he can. Be sure that you have puppy-proofed every inch of the interior (and exterior) of your home.

PUPPY-PROOFING YOUR HOME

Aside from making sure that your Briard will be comfortable in your home, you also have to make sure that your home is safe for your Briard. This means taking precautions so that your pup will not get into anything he should not get into and that there is nothing within his reach that may harm him should he sniff it, chew it, inspect it, etc. This probably seems obvious since, while you are primarily concerned with your pup's safety, at the same time you do not want your belongings to be ruined. Breakables should be placed out of reach if your dog is to have full run of the house. If he is to be limited to certain places within the house, keep any potentially dangerous items in the 'off-limits' areas. An electrical cord can pose a danger should the puppy try to taste it—and who is going to convince a pup that it would not make a great chew toy? Cords should be fastened tightly against the wall.

It is also important to make sure that the outside of your house is safe. Of course, your puppy should never be left unsupervised, but a pup let loose in the garden will want to run and explore, and he should be granted that freedom. Do not let a fence give you a false sense of security; you would be surprised how crafty (and persistent) a puppy can be in working out how to dig

CHOOSE AN APPROPRIATE COLLAR

The **BUCKLE COLLAR** is the standard collar used for everyday purposes. Be sure that you adjust the buckle on growing puppies. Check it every day. It can become too tight overnight! These collars can be made of leather or nylon. Attach your dog's identification tags to this collar.

The **CHOKE COLLAR** is made for training. It is constructed of highly polished steel so that it slides easily through the stainless steel loop. The idea is that the dog controls the pressure around its neck and he will stop pulling if the collar becomes uncomfortable. It is never left on a dog when not training. Choke collars are inappropriate for Briards, as the coat will be destroyed.

The **HALTER** is for a trained dog that has to be restrained to prevent running away, chasing a cat and the like. Considered the most humane of all devices, it is frequently used on smaller dogs for which collars are not comfortable. The halter is inappropriate for the Briard as well, as it also will destroy the coat.

under and squeeze his way
through small holes, or to jump or
climb over a fence. The remedy is
to make the fence high enough so
that it really is impossible for
your dog to get over it (about 2 to
3 metres should suffice), and well
embedded into the ground.

Be sure to repair or secure any
gaps in the fence. Check the fence
periodically to ensure that it is in
good shape and make repairs as
needed; a very determined pup
may return to the same spot to
'work on it' until he is able to get
through.

FIRST TRIP TO THE VET
You have picked out your puppy,
and your home and family are
ready. Now all you have to do is
collect your Briard from the
breeder and the fun begins, right?
Well…not so fast. Something else
you need to prepare is your pup's
first trip to the veterinary surgeon.

Give the Briard safe toys to distract him from finding too much mischief when he is outdoors.

NATURAL TOXINS
Examine your grass and garden
landscaping before bringing your
puppy home. Many varieties of
plants have leaves, stems or flowers
that are toxic if ingested, and you
can depend on a curious puppy to
investigate them. Ask your vet for
information on poisonous plants or
research them at your library.

Perhaps the breeder can
recommend someone in the area,
or maybe you know some other
Briard owners who can suggest a
good vet. Either way, you should
have an appointment arranged for
your pup before you pick him up
and plan on taking him for an
examination before bringing him
home.

The pup's first visit will
consist of an overall examination
to make sure that the pup does
not have any problems that are
not apparent to you. The veterinary surgeon will also set up a
schedule for the pup's
vaccinations; the breeder will
inform you of which ones the pup
has already received and the vet
can continue from there.

INTRODUCTION TO THE FAMILY
Everyone in the house will be
excited about the puppy's coming
home and will want to pet him
and play with him, but it is best

PUPPY-PROOFING

Remember to thoroughly puppy-proof your house before bringing your puppy home. Never use vermin poisons in any area accessible to the puppy. Avoid the use of toilet bowl cleaners. Most dogs are born with 'toilet bowl sonar,' and they often make a beeline there—and the Briard will be tall enough to drink from the bowl in no time! Rubbish bins are also very popular with Briards.

to make the introduction low-key so as not to overwhelm the puppy. He is apprehensive already. It is the first time he has been separated from his mother and his breeder, and the ride to your home is likely the first time he has been in a car. The last thing you want to do is smother him, as this will only frighten him further. This is not to say that human contact is not extremely necessary at this stage, because this is the time when a connection between the pup and his human family is formed. Gentle petting and soothing words should help console him, as well as just putting him down and letting him explore on his own (under your watchful eye, of course).

The pup may approach the family members or may busy himself with exploring for a while. Gradually, each person should spend some time with the pup, one at a time, crouching down to get as close to the pup's level as possible and letting him sniff each family member's hands and petting him gently. He definitely needs human attention and he needs to be touched—this is how to form an immediate bond. Just remember that the pup is experiencing a lot of things for the first time, at the same time. There are new people, new noises, new smells, and new things to investigate, so be gentle, be affectionate and be as comforting as you can.

YOUR PUP'S FIRST NIGHT HOME

You have travelled home with your new charge safely in his crate or on a friend's lap. He's been to the vet for a thorough check-up; he's been weighed, his papers examined; perhaps he's even been vaccinated and wormed as well. He's met the whole family

Briards will sniff and search everything, so never leave anything potentially harmful for the snooping Briard.

PROPER SOCIALISATION

The socialisation period for puppies is from age 8 to 16 weeks. This is the time when puppies need to leave their birth family and take up residence with their new owners, where they will meet many new people, other pets, etc. Failure to be adequately socialised can cause the dog to grow up fearing others and being shy and unfriendly due to a lack of self-confidence.

and licked the whole family, including the excited children and the less-than-happy cat. He's explored his area, his new bed, the garden and anywhere else he's been permitted. He's eaten his first meal at home and relieved himself in the proper place. He's heard lots of new sounds, smelled new friends and seen more of the outside world than ever before, and that was just the first day!

He's worn out and is ready for bed...or so you think!

It's puppy's first night and you are ready to say 'Good night'— keep in mind that this is the puppy's first night ever to be sleeping alone. His dam and litter-mates are no longer at paw's length and he's a bit scared, cold and lonely. Be reassuring to your new family member. This is not the time to spoil him and give in to his inevitable whining.

Puppies whine. They whine to let others know where they are and hopefully to get company out of it. Place your pup in his new bed...in his room and close the door. Mercifully, he may fall asleep without a peep. When the inevitable occurs, ignore the whining: he is fine. Be strong and keep his interest in mind. Do not allow your heart to become guilty and visit the pup. He will fall asleep.

Many breeders recommend placing a piece of bedding from his former home in his new bed so that he recognises the scent of his littermates. Others still advise placing a hot water bottle in his bed for warmth. This latter may be a good idea provided the pup doesn't attempt to suckle—he'll get good and wet and may not fall asleep so fast.

Pup's first night can be somewhat stressful for the pup and his new family. Remember that you are setting the tone of nighttime at your house. Unless you want to play with your pup every evening at 10 p.m., midnight and 2 a.m., don't initiate the habit. Your family will thank you, and so will your pup!

PREVENTING PUPPY PROBLEMS

SOCIALISATION

Now that you have done all of the preparatory work and have helped your pup get accustomed to his new home and family, it is about time for you to have some fun! Socialising your Briard pup gives you the opportunity to show off your new friend, and your pup gets to reap the benefits of being an adorable furry creature that people will want to pet and, in general, think is absolutely precious!

Besides getting to know his new family, your puppy should be exposed to other people, animals and situations, but, of course, he must not come into close contact with dogs you don't know well until his course of injections is fully complete. Socialisation will help him become well adjusted as he grows up and less prone to being timid or fearful of the new things he will encounter. Your pup's socialisation began at his breeder's, but now it is your responsibility to continue it. The socialisation he receives up until the age of 12 weeks is the most

critical, as this is the time when he forms his impressions of the outside world. Special care should be taken during the eight-to-ten-week-old period, also known as the fear period. The interaction he receives during this time should be gentle and reassuring. Lack of

MANNERS MATTER

During the socialisation process, a puppy should meet people, experience different environments and definitely be exposed to other canines. Through playing and interacting with other dogs, your puppy will learn lessons, ranging from controlling the pressure of his jaws by biting his littermates to the inner-workings of the canine pack, which he will apply to his human relationships for the rest of his life. That is why removing a puppy from its litter too early (before eight weeks) can be detrimental to the pup's development.

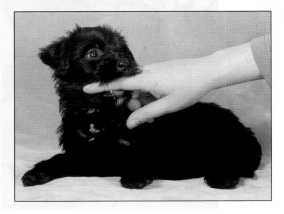

socialisation can manifest itself in fear and aggression as the dog grows up. He needs lots of human contact, affection, handling and exposure to other animals.

MEET THE WORLD

Thorough socialisation includes not only meeting new people but also being introduced to new experiences such as riding in the car, having his coat brushed, hearing the television, walking in a crowd—the list is endless. The more your pup experiences, and the more positive the experiences are, the less of a shock and the less frightening it will be for your pup to encounter new things.

Once your pup has received his necessary vaccinations, feel free to take him out and about (on his lead of course). Walk him around the neighbourhood, take him on your daily errands, let him meet other dogs and pets, etc. Puppies do not have to try to make friends; there will be no shortage of people who will want to introduce themselves. Just make sure that you carefully supervise each meeting. If the neighbourhood children want to say hello, for example, that is great—children and pups most often make great companions. However, sometimes an excited child can unintentionally handle a pup too roughly, or an

who becomes leader and who becomes the 'pack' is entirely up to you! Your pup's intuitive quest for dominance, coupled with the fact that it is nearly impossible to look at a Briard pup, with his 'bunny ears' and 'wolf nose,' and not cave in, give the pup almost an unfair advantage in getting the upper hand.

A pup will definitely test the waters to see what he can and cannot do. Do not give in to those pleading eyes—stand your ground when it comes to disciplining the pup and make sure that all family members do the same. It will only confuse the pup when mother tells him to get off the sofa when

Socialisation of your Briard should be undertaken while it is still a puppy. He should meet other dogs and other people and become accustomed to traffic noises and walking on a lead.

overzealous pup can playfully nip a little too hard. You want to make socialisation experiences positive ones. What a pup learns during this very formative stage will impact his attitude toward future encounters. You want your dog to be comfortable around everyone. A pup that has had a bad experience with a child may grow up to be a dog that is shy around or aggressive towards children.

CONSISTENCY IN TRAINING
Dogs, being pack animals, naturally need a leader, or else they try to establish dominance in their packs. When you bring a dog into your family, the choice of

A FORTNIGHT'S GRACE
It will take at least two weeks for your puppy to become accustomed to his new surroundings. Give him lots of love, attention, handling, frequent opportunities to relieve himself, a diet he likes to eat and a place he can call his own.

It will seem for the first few months that your Briard puppy's brains are in his mouth—all he can think about is chewing. Discourage the pup from chewing on your shoes, no matter how amusing you find it!

he is used to sitting there with father to watch the nightly news. Avoid discrepancies by having all members of the household decide the rules before the pup even comes home...and be consistent in enforcing them! Early training shapes the dog's personality, so you cannot be unclear in what you expect.

COMMON PUPPY PROBLEMS
The best way to prevent puppy problems is to be proactive in stopping an undesirable behaviour as soon as it starts. The old saying 'You can't teach an old dog new tricks' does not necessarily hold true, but it is true that it is much easier to discourage bad behaviour in a young developing pup than to wait until the pup's bad behaviour becomes the adult dog's bad habit. There are some problems that are especially prevalent in puppies as they develop.

NIPPING
As puppies start to teethe, they feel the need to sink their teeth into anything available...unfortunately that includes your fingers, arms, hair and toes. You may find this behaviour cute for the first five seconds...until you feel just how sharp those puppy teeth are. This is something you want to discourage immediately and consistently with a firm 'No!' (or whatever number of firm 'No's' it takes for him to understand that you mean business). Then replace your finger with an appropriate chew toy. While this behaviour is merely annoying when the dog is young, it can become dangerous as your Briard's adult teeth grow in and his jaws develop, and he continues to think it is okay to gnaw on human appendages. Your Briard does not mean any harm with a friendly nip, but he also does not know his own strength.

THE RIDE HOME
Taking your dog from the breeder to your home in a car can be a very uncomfortable experience for both of you. The puppy will have been taken from his warm, friendly, safe environment and brought into a strange new environment—an environment that moves! Be prepared for loose bowels, urination, crying, whining and even fear biting. With proper love and encouragement when you arrive home, the stress of the trip should quickly disappear.

CRYING/WHINING

Your pup will often cry, whine, whimper, howl or make some type of commotion when he is left alone. This is basically his way of calling out for attention to make sure that you know he is there and you have not forgotten about him. He feels insecure when he is left alone, when you are out of the house and he is in his bed, or when you are in another part of the house and he cannot see you. The noise he is making is an expression of the anxiety he feels at being alone, so he needs to be taught that being alone is okay. You are not actually training the dog to stop making noise, you are training him to feel comfortable when he is alone and thus removing the need for him to make the noise. This is where the bed with cosy bedding and a favourite toy comes in handy. You want to know that he is safe when you are not there to supervise, either in a secure run in the garden or shut in one of the rooms that are puppy-proofed.

Accustom the pup to being alone in short, gradually increasing time intervals in which you put him into bed, maybe with a treat, and stay in the room with him. If he cries or makes a fuss, do not go to him, but stay in his sight. Gradually he will realise that staying in his bed is all right without your help, and it will not be so traumatic for him when you

are not around. You may want to leave the radio on softly when you leave the house; the sound of human voices may be comforting to him.

CHEWING TIPS

Chewing goes hand in hand with nipping in the sense that a teething puppy is always looking for a way to soothe his aching gums. In this case, instead of chewing on you, he may have taken a liking to your favourite shoe or something else that he should not be chewing. Again, realise that this is a normal canine behaviour that does not need to be discouraged, only redirected. Your pup just needs to be taught what is acceptable to chew on and what is off limits. Consistently tell him NO when you catch him chewing on something forbidden and give him a chew toy. Conversely, praise him when you catch him chewing on something appropriate. In this way you are discouraging the inappropriate behaviour and reinforcing the desired behaviour. The puppy chewing should stop after his adult teeth have come in, but an adult dog continues to chew for various reasons—perhaps because he is bored or needs to relieve tension. That is why it is important to redirect his chewing when he is still young.

DIETARY AND FEEDING CONSIDERATIONS

Today the choices of food for your Briard are many and varied. There are simply dozens of brands of food in all sorts of flavours and textures, ranging from puppy diets to those for seniors. There are even hypoallergenic and low-calorie diets available. Because your Briard's food has a bearing on coat, health, temperament and, most especially, on the development of the bones of the puppy, it is essential that the most suitable diet is selected for a Briard of his age. It is fair to say, however, that even dedicated owners can be somewhat perplexed by the enormous range of foods available. Only understanding what is best for your dog will help you reach a valued decision.

Dog foods are produced in three basic types: dried, semi-moist and tinned. The bottom-of-the-range dried foods are useful for the cost-conscious, for they are less expensive than semi-moist or tinned. These contain the least fat and the most preservatives, unlike the top-of-the-range dried foods, which are really quite expensive but provide high-quality food in low bulk form.

In general, tinned foods are made up of 60–70 percent water, while semi-moist ones often contain so much sugar that they are perhaps the least preferred by owners, even though their dogs seem to like them.

When selecting your dog's diet, three stages of development must be considered: the puppy stage, the adult stage and the senior or veteran stage.

PUPPY STAGE

Puppies instinctively want to suck milk from their mother's teats and a normal puppy will exhibit this behaviour from just a few moments after birth. If puppies do not attempt to suckle within the first half-hour or so, they should be encouraged to do so by placing them on the nipples. The first fluid produced by the bitch after whelping is a yellowish substance called colostrum, which contains a high concentration of antibodies to protect the puppies from infection during the first eight to ten weeks of their lives. Although a mother's milk is much better than any milk formula, despite there being some excellent ones available, if the puppies do not feed, the breeder will have to feed them himself. For breeders with less experience, advice from a veterinary surgeon is important so that not only the right quantity of milk is fed but also that of correct quality, fed at suitably frequent intervals, usually every two hours during the first few days of life.

Puppies should be allowed to nurse from their mothers for about the first six weeks, although from the third or fourth week the breeder begins to introduce small portions of solid food. Most breeders like to introduce alternate milk and meat meals initially, building up to weaning time.

By the time the puppies are seven or a maximum of eight weeks old, they should be fully weaned and fed solely on a proprietary puppy food. Selection of the most suitable, good-quality diet at this time is essential, for a puppy's fastest growth rate is

DO DOGS HAVE TASTE BUDS?

Watching a dog 'wolf' or gobble his food, seemingly without chewing, leads an owner to wonder whether their dogs can taste anything. Yes, dogs have taste buds, with sensory perception of sweet, salty and sour. Puppies are born with fully mature taste buds.

during the first year of life. Veterinary surgeons are usually able to offer advice in this regard and, although the frequency of meals are reduced over time, only when a young dog has reached the age of about 18 months should an adult diet be fed.

Puppy and junior diets should be well balanced for the needs of your dog, so that except in certain circumstances additional vitamins, minerals and proteins will not be required, and indeed can sometimes be harmful.

Feeding the adult Briard will not present a challenge to the owner once a suitable high-quality dried food is selected.

ADULT DIETS

A dog is considered an adult when it has stopped growing, so in general the diet of a Briard can be changed to an adult one at about 18 months of age. Again you should rely upon your veterinary surgeon to recommend an acceptable maintenance diet. Major dog food manufacturers specialise in this type of food, and it is necessary for you to select the one best suited to your dog's needs. Active dogs have different requirements than sedentary ones.

SENIOR DIETS

As dogs get older their metabolism changes. The older dog usually exercises less, moves

DIETARY INFORMATION

Follow the manufacturer's advice about amounts to feed your dog. Most of the major dog food companies employ feeding consultants who will answer telephone or written questions, and many have websites through which you can send questions by e-mail. Your vet is another good source of dietary information.

It is very easy to ruin your puppy by incorrect feeding; by 'ruin,' I mean to cause it to grow up with deformed bones. It is hard to feed a small dog incorrectly, but a larger breed like the Briard needs exactly the right amount of nutrients, and especially minerals like calcium.

A vet will heave a sigh of relief if you tell them that you are going to feed a top-quality food, following the manufacturer's advice, as it is very unlikely that your dog will experience problems.

more slowly and sleeps more. This change in lifestyle and physiological performance requires a change in diet. Since these changes take place slowly, they might not be recognisable. In most breeds, what is easily recognisable is weight gain. By continuing to feed your dog an adult maintenance diet when it is slowing down metabolically, your dog will gain weight. Any extra weight will compound the health problems that already accompany old age, so try to regulate the food intake with the amount of energy output so that reducing diets are unnecessary.

As your dog gets older, few of his organs function up to par. The kidneys slow down and the liver becomes less efficient. These age-related factors are best handled with a change in diet and a change in feeding schedule to give smaller portions that are more easily digested.

There is no single best diet for every older dog. While many dogs do well on light or senior diets, other dogs do better on other special premium diets such as lamb and rice. I do not think that it is safe to give old dogs puppy food as this has a very high protein content that the older liver and kidneys cannot cope with. Be sensitive to your senior Briard's diet and this will help control other problems that may arise with your old friend.

What are you feeding your dog?

Read the label on your dog food. Many dog foods only advise what 50—55% of the contents are, leaving the other 45% in doubt.

Calcium 1.3%
Fatty Acids 1.6%
Crude Fibre 4.6%
Moisture 11%
Crude Fat 14%
Crude Protein 22%
45.5% ? ? ?

BLOAT PREVENTATIVE

Gastric torsion, or bloat, is a killer of Briards, and the research does link its incidence to the diet fed. Never feed cheap grain-based food, as this swells greatly in the stomach and is dangerous. Before buying a brand of complete diet, test one piece in a glass of water. Most manufacturers are happy to let you have a small free sample. If the bit of food swells, do not buy it. If after soaking for half an hour or so it is the same size, then it is suitable to allow your Briard to taste it. Whatever happens in the glass mirrors what will happen in the dog's stomach when filled with digestive acid.

WATER

Just as your dog needs proper nutrition from his food, water is an essential 'nutrient' as well. Water keeps the body properly hydrated and promotes normal function of the body's systems. During house-training, it is necessary to keep an eye on how much water your Briard is drinking, but once he is reliably trained he should have access to clean fresh water at all times. Make sure the dog's water bowl is clean, and change the water often, making sure that water is always available for your dog, especially if you feed dried food.

EXERCISE

PUPPIES

A Briard has a fair amount of growing to do going from puppyhood to adulthood. Most of this seems to be done when the puppy is sleeping, and sleep and rest are vital to the growing puppy. Exercise should be limited when your Briard is small, but once the leg bones have finished growing, at roughly a year of age, your Briard is able to manage much more exercise. The last bones to stop growing are the skull bones, but this does not have a bearing on the exercise regime you create for your dog.

ADULT DOGS

Although an adult Briard is large, it does not always need miles and miles of walking daily. However, a sedentary lifestyle is as harmful to a dog as it is to a person. Regular walks, play sessions in the garden or letting the adult dog run free in the securely fenced garden under supervision are the best forms of exercise. Getting into a routine of a daily lengthy walk, no matter what the weather, is the best way to keep your Briard at his fittest. If you have a 'couch potato,' increase the exercise slowly. Not only is exercise essential to keep the dog's body fit, it is essential to his mental well-being as well. A bored dog will find something to do, which often manifests itself in some type of destructive behaviour. In this sense, it is essential for the owner's mental well-being as well!

GROOMING

Your Briard will need to be groomed regularly, so it is essential that brief grooming sessions are introduced from a very early age. From the very beginning, a few minutes each day should be set aside for grooming. Increase the duration of the sessions, building up slowly as the puppy matures and the coat grows in length. Though a puppy is initially quite small, and small dogs are usually groomed on tables, it is not long until the gangly adolescent is far too big to be put on a table safely.

Start brushing by introducing a few gentle brush strokes. Be sure not to tug at any knots at this stage, for this would cause the puppy to associate grooming with pain. This may take a little getting used to for both you and your puppy. Not only does the coat get longer with age, allowing more tangles to form behind the ears and elbows and in the trousers, but also the coat will change from the fluffier puppy coat to the silkier adult one.

You will certainly need to groom the coat between bath times, and it is best to moisten it either with a spray of water or a light conditioning spray.

DRINK, DRANK, DRUNK— MAKE IT A DOUBLE

In both humans and dogs, as well as most living organisms, water forms the major part of nearly every body tissue. Naturally, we take water for granted, but without it, life as we know it would cease.

For dogs, water is needed to keep their bodies functioning biochemically. Additionally, water is needed to replace the water lost while panting. Unlike humans, who are able to sweat to dissipate heat, dogs must pant to cool down, thereby losing the vital water from their bodies needed to regulate their body temperatures. Humans lose electrolyte-containing products and other body-fluid components through sweating; dogs do not lose anything except water.

Water is essential always, but especially so when the weather is hot or humid or when your dog is exercising or working vigorously.

Routine Grooming

Initially the coat should be brushed section by section in the direction of coat growth. It is imperative to groom right down to the skin so that the undercoat is not left matted. The best brush to use is a good-quality bristle brush; a better quality brush will cost more money, but will generally do a better job.

If you do find a mat in the coat, spray the mat with a generous amount of conditioning or anti-tangle spray. Leave this to soak in for a few moments, then gently tease out the mat with your fingers. Always work from the inside out or the knot will just get tighter! Be careful not to tug at the knot—it will be painful for the pup, and will also pull out too much coat.

THE BEST GROOMING TOOL

Pet shops and grooming stands at dog shows sell many different types of brushes and combs. For a Briard, the best tool is a quality real bristle brush, although cheaper bristle brushes are quite acceptable. The combs that look like something left over from a mediaeval torture kit will destroy and pull out your dog's coat. Make sure that your name is on your top-quality bristle brush, as it is such a valued and valuable item that it may go missing.

Take care in grooming the tummy and under the 'armpits,' for these areas are especially sensitive. There is really no harm in cutting away small tight knots

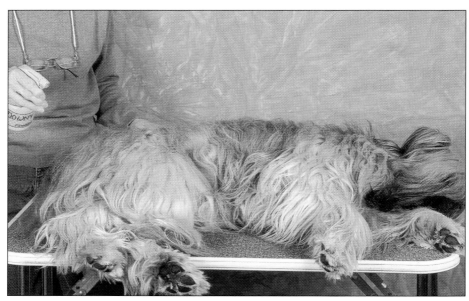

A grooming table makes the chore of grooming the Briard's coat more manageable. Since the Briard is such a large dog, with an abundant coat, grooming is a time-consuming venture.

from under the armpits, as these will not show and the dog will feel more comfortable. However, a Briard in show coat should not be trimmed, so scissors should only be used when absolutely necessary. Trimming below the pads of the feet prevents uncomfortable hairballs from forming between the pads.

An area that will need special attention is the hair behind the ear. This hair is often of a softer texture and knots easily.

The trousers of a Briard are heavily coated and will also need regular grooming. To prevent knots and tangles, be sure to remove any debris that may have accumulated following a visit outdoors. Also, always check your dog's back end to see that nothing remains attached to the coat from his relieving himself. Between baths you may like to use a damp sponge, but always be sure to dry the coat thoroughly. Drying will help to keep the dog comfortable.

Make checking the eyes, ears and feet part of the regular grooming routine. If needed, the eyes can be cleaned using a canine liquid eye cleaner; a special cleaner is also available for cleaning the ears. Pay attention to the feet: be sure you don't allow knots to build up between the toes, and always keep an eye on the length of the toenails.

SOAP IT UP
The use of human soap products like shampoo, bubble bath and hand soap can be damaging to a dog's coat and skin. Human products are too strong; they remove the protective oils coating the dog's hair and skin that make him water-resistant. Use only shampoo made especially for dogs. You may like to use a medicated shampoo, which will help to keep external parasites at bay.

BATHING AND DRYING
How frequently you decide to bath your Briard will depend very much whether your dog is a show dog or a pet. Show dogs are usually bathed before every show, which may be as frequent as once a week. Pet dogs are usually bathed much less frequently.

Every owner has his own preference as to how best to bath, but ideally the coat should be groomed through before bathing. It should make things less slippery and dangerous to use a non-slip mat in the bath. Once the dog has been lifted in, wet the coat thoroughly using a shower attachment. It is imperative that the water temperature is tested on your own hand before spraying the dog. Use a good-quality shampoo designed especially for dogs, always stroking, rather than rubbing, it into the coat so as not to create knots. When the

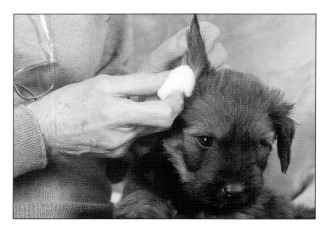

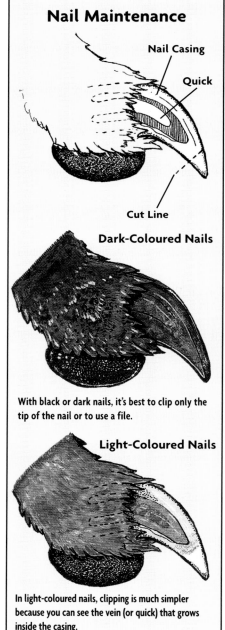

Nail Maintenance

Nail Casing

Quick

Cut Line

Dark-Coloured Nails

With black or dark nails, it's best to clip only the tip of the nail or to use a file.

Light-Coloured Nails

In light-coloured nails, clipping is much simpler because you can see the vein (or quick) that grows inside the casing.

Keep your dog's ears clean with a piece of cotton wool and a cleaner available from your vet or pet-supply outlet.

shampoo has been thoroughly rinsed out, apply a canine conditioner in the same manner, then rinse again until the water runs clear. Many people like to use a baby shampoo on the head to avoid irritation to the eyes, and some like to plug the ears with cotton wool to avoid water getting inside them.

Before taking your dog out of the bath, it is a good idea to try to use a particularly absorbent towel to soak up excess moisture. As a Briard can get himself out of the bath more easily than many breeds, often a soaking wet dog will bounce out to shake and cover the room in water before it is possible to get the towel ready.

The best finish for the show ring is given by using a blaster on the coat, but this has to be introduced when the Briard is a puppy as it can be frightening to have a hot, noisy machine so close.

Work systematically, all the while brushing as well as applying warm air from the hair dryer. Put the finishing touches to your dog's coat, just as you would do when grooming without a bath. Bathing and grooming a long-coated breed is always a lengthy task, but the end result will make it all worthwhile.

EAR CLEANING

The ears should be kept clean, and this can be done with a piece of cotton wool and special cleaner or ear powder made especially for dogs. Never stick anything into the ear further than you can see. Be on the lookout for any signs of infection or ear mite infestation. If your Briard has been shaking his head or scratching at his ears frequently, this usually indicates a problem. If his ears have an unusual odour, this is a sure sign of mite infestation or infection, and a signal to have his ears checked by the veterinary surgeon.

NAIL CLIPPING

Your Briard should be accustomed to having his nails trimmed at an early age, since it will be part of your maintenance routine throughout his life. Long sharp nails can scratch someone unintentionally, and they deform the foot by making the toes splay outwards. Also, a long nail has a better chance of ripping and

PEDICURE TIP

A dog that spends a lot of time outside on an hard surface, such as cement or pavement, will have his nails naturally worn down and may not need to have them trimmed as often, except maybe in the colder months when he is not outside as much. Regardless, it is best to get your dog accustomed to the nail-trimming procedure at an early age so that he is used to it. Some dogs are especially sensitive about having their feet touched, but if a dog has experienced it since puppy-hood, it should not bother him.

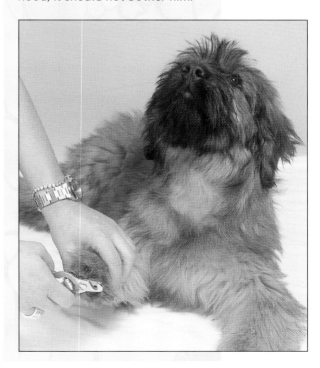

DEADLY DECAY
Did you know that periodontal disease (a condition of the bone and gums surrounding a tooth) can be fatal? Having your dog's teeth and mouth checked yearly can prevent it.

bleeding. A good rule of thumb is that if you can hear your dog's nails' clicking on the floor when he walks, his nails are too long.

Before you start cutting, make sure you can identify the 'quick' in each nail. The quick is formed by the blood vessels that run through the centre of each nail and are found rather close to the end. The quick will bleed if accidentally cut, which will be quite painful for the dog as it also contains nerve endings. Keep some type of clotting agent on hand, such as a styptic pencil or styptic powder (the type used for shaving). This will stop the bleeding quickly when applied to

the end of the cut nail. Pressure on the nail also stops bleeding. Do not panic if this happens, just stop the bleeding and talk soothingly to your dog.

Hold your pup steady as you begin trimming his nails; you do not want him to make any sudden movements or run away. Talk to him soothingly and stroke him as you clip. Holding his foot in your hand, simply take off the end of each nail in one quick clip. You can purchase nail clippers that are specially made for dogs; you can probably find them wherever you buy pet or grooming supplies.

TRAVELLING WITH YOUR DOG

Car Travel
You should accustom your Briard to riding in a car at an early age. You may or may not take him in the car often, but at the very least he will need to go to the vet and you do not want these trips to be traumatic for the dog or troublesome for you.

As a puppy, a Briard can sit on the lap of a passenger while you drive. Another option, especially when he starts to grow, is a specially made safety harness for dogs, which straps the dog in much like a seat belt. Do not let the dog roam loose in the vehicle—this is very dangerous. If you should stop suddenly, your dog can be thrown and injured. If the dog starts climbing on you and pestering you while you are driving, you will not be able to concentrate on the road. It is an unsafe situation for everyone— human and canine.

For longer trips, be prepared to stop to let the dog relieve himself. Bring along whatever you need to clean up after him. You should take along some paper kitchen towels and perhaps some old towelling for use should he have a toileting accident in the car or suffer from travel sickness.

AIR TRAVEL

While it is possible to take a dog on a flight within Britain, this is fairly unusual and advance permission is always required. The dog will be required to travel in a fibreglass crate and you should always check in advance with the airline regarding specific requirements. To help the dog be at ease, put one of his favourite toys and a familiar blanket in the crate with him. Do not feed the dog for at least six hours before the trip to minimise his need to relieve himself. However, certain regulations specify that water must be made available to the dog in the crate. Make sure that your dog is properly identified and that your contact information appears on his ID tags and on his crate. Animals travel in a different area of the plane to that where the human travellers are, so every rule must be strictly followed to

prevent the risk of getting separated from your dog.

BOARDING

So you want to take a family holiday—and you want to include *all* members of the family. You would probably make arrangements for accommodation ahead of time anyway, but this is especially important when travelling with a large dog. You do not want to make an overnight stop at the only place around for miles and find out that they do not allow dogs. Also, you do not want to reserve a place for your family without confirming that you are travelling with a dog, because if it against their policy you may not have a place to stay.

Alternatively, if you are travelling and choose not to bring your

Owning a Briard (or two) requires that you have a suitable vehicle to travel with the dogs. Crates and special divider gates make travelling convenient and safe for Briards and owners alike.

Select a top-rate boarding kennel before you actually need one. Be sure it is clean, convenient and properly staffed, offering the dogs regular exercise and attention.

Briard, you will have to make arrangements for him while you are away. Some options are to take him to a neighbour's house to stay while you are gone, to have a trusted neighbour stay at your house or to bring your dog to a reputable boarding kennel. For large dogs, personal recommendation is the best way to find a kennel. Sometimes your dog's breeder will take your Briard while you are away on holiday, if they do not live too far away, or another dog owner can look after him.

If you choose to board him at a kennel, you should visit in advance to see the facility, how clean they are and where the dogs are kept. Talk to some of the employees, see how they treat the dogs and make some enquiries—are they familiar with large breeds, have they experience in grooming long-coated dogs, do they spend time with the dogs, play with them, exercise them, etc.? Also find out the kennel's policy on vaccinations and what they require. This is for all of the dogs' safety, since when dogs are kept together there is a greater risk of diseases' being passed from dog to dog. Do not board your Briard in a place that does not ask to see your vaccination certificates.

IDENTIFICATION
Your Briard is your valued companion and friend. That is

why you always keep a close eye on him and you have made sure that he cannot escape from the garden or wriggle out of his collar to chase something. However, accidents can happen and there may come a time when your dog unexpectedly gets separated from you. If this unfortunate event should occur, the first thing on your mind will be finding him. Proper identification, including an ID tag and possibly a microchip will increase the chances of his being returned to you safely and quickly.

IDENTIFICATION OPTIONS

As puppies become more and more expensive, especially those puppies of high quality for showing and/or breeding, they have a greater chance of being stolen. The usual collar dog tag is, of course, easily removed. But there are two more permanent techniques that have become widely used for identification.

The puppy microchip implantation involves the injection of a small microchip, about the size of a corn kernel, under the skin of the dog. If your dog shows up at a clinic or shelter, or is offered for resale under less than savoury circumstances, it can be positively identified by the microchip. The microchip is scanned, and a registry quickly identifies you as the owner. This is not only protection against theft, but should the dog run away or go chasing a squirrel and become lost, you have a fair chance of his being returned to you.

Tattooing is done on various parts of the dog, from his belly to his cheeks. The number tattooed can be your telephone number or any other number that you can easily memorise. When professional dog thieves see a tattooed dog, they usually lose interest. Both microchipping and tattooing can be done at your local veterinary clinic. For the safety of our dogs, no laboratory facility or dog broker will accept a tattooed dog as stock.

Your Briard should always be wearing a proper identification tag on a light but sturdy collar.

Living with an untrained dog is a lot like owning a piano that you do not know how to play—it is a nice object to look at, but it does not do much more than that to bring you pleasure. Now try taking piano lessons, and suddenly the piano becomes alive and brings forth magical sounds and rhythms that set your heart singing and your body swaying.

The same is true with your Briard. Any dog is a big responsibility and, if not trained sensibly, may develop unacceptable behaviour that annoys you or could even be dangerous.

To train your Briard, you may like to enrol both of you in an obedience class. At the class, it will be easier to teach him good manners with the support of others as you learn how and why he behaves in the ways that he does. Find out how to communicate with your dog and how to recognise and understand his communications with you. Suddenly the dog takes a new role in your life—he is smart, interesting, well behaved and fun to be with. He demonstrates his bond of devotion to you daily. In other words, your Briard does wonders for your ego because he

constantly reminds you that you are his leader.

Those involved with teaching dog obedience and counselling owners about their dogs' behaviour have discovered some interesting facts about dog ownership. For example, training dogs when they are puppies results in the highest rate of success in developing well-mannered and well-adjusted adult dogs. Training an older dog, from six months to six years of age, can produce almost equal results providing that the owner accepts the dog's slower rate of learning capability and is willing to work patiently to help the dog succeed at developing to his fullest potential. Unfortunately, many owners of untrained adult dogs lack the patience factor, so they do not persist until their dogs are successful at learning particular behaviours.

Training a puppy, aged 10 to 16 weeks (20 weeks at the most), is like working with a dry sponge in a pool of water. The pup soaks up whatever you show him and constantly looks for more things to do and learn. At this early age, his body is not yet producing sexual hormones, and therein lies

OBEDIENCE SCHOOL

Taking your dog to an obedience school may be the best investment in time and money you can ever make. You will enjoy the benefits for the lifetime of your dog and you will have the opportunity to meet people who have similar expectations for their companion dogs.

the reason for such a high rate of success, along with the fact that he is at the stage in his life when his mother and the other pack members would be teaching him the survival skills he would need to live in the wild were he not a member of a domesticated species. Without hormones, he is focused on you and your family as the surrogate pack and not particularly interested in investigating other places, dogs, people, etc. without your support. You are his leader: his provider of food, water, shelter and security. He latches onto you and wants to stay close. He will usually follow you from room to room, will not let you out of his sight when you are outdoors with him and will respond in like manner to the people and animals you encounter. If you greet a friend warmly, a young Briard will be happy to greet that person as well. If, however, you are hesitant or anxious about the approach of a stranger, he will

respond accordingly.

Once the puppy begins to produce sexual hormones, he begins to investigate the wider world around him. It is at this time that you may notice that the untrained dog begins to wander away from you and ignore your commands to stay close even more than usual.

There are usually training classes within a reasonable distance of your home, but you can also do a lot to train your dog yourself. And it is the time spent

You will need to have your Briard's complete attention whenever undergoing any training. Adult dogs are more difficult to train, but, if the owner places emphasis on follow-through for all commands, success is usually met.

during the week practising at home, outside the class environment, that is the real learning time.

This chapter is devoted to helping you train your Briard at home. If the recommended procedures are followed faithfully, you may expect positive results that will prove rewarding to both you and your dog.

Whether your new charge is a puppy or a mature adult, the methods of teaching and the techniques we use in training basic behaviours are the same. After all, no dog, whether puppy or adult, likes harsh or inhumane methods. All creatures, however, respond to gentle motivational methods and sincere praise and encouragement. Now let us get started.

HOUSE-TRAINING

You can train a puppy to relieve itself wherever you choose, but this must be somewhere suitable. You should bear in mind from the outset that when your puppy is old enough to go out in public places, any canine deposits must be removed at once. You will always have to carry with you a small plastic bag or 'poop-scoop'. Outdoor training includes such surfaces as grass, soil or cement. Indoor training usually means training your dog to use newspaper, although this is not the best option with a large dog

like the Briard.

When deciding on the surface and location that you will want your Briard to use, be sure it is going to be permanent. Training your dog to grass and then changing your mind two months later is extremely difficult for both dog and owner.

Next, choose the command you will use each and every time you want your puppy to void. 'Hurry up' and 'Toilet' are examples of commands commonly used by dog owners. Get in the habit of giving your chosen relief command before you take him out. That way, when he becomes an adult, you will be able to determine if he wants to go out when you ask him. A confirmation will be signs of interest, wagging his tail, watching you intently, going to the door, etc.

PUPPY'S NEEDS

Puppy needs to relieve himself after play periods, after each meal, after he has been sleeping and at any time he indicates that he is looking for a place to urinate or defecate. Urine and faeces are kept inside because of circular muscles called sphincters. The control over these muscles is not fully developed in very young puppies. Therefore, just like human babies, puppies need to relieve themselves frequently.

Take your puppy out often—

CANINE DEVELOPMENT SCHEDULE

It is important to understand how and at what age a puppy develops into adulthood.
If you are a puppy owner, consult the following Canine Development Schedule to
determine the stage of development your puppy is currently experiencing.
This knowledge will help you as you work with the puppy in the weeks and months ahead.

Period	Age	Characteristics
FIRST TO THIRD	BIRTH TO SEVEN WEEKS	Puppy needs food, sleep and warmth, and responds to simple and gentle touching. Needs mother for security and disciplining. Needs littermates for learning and interacting with other dogs. Pup learns to function within a pack and learns pack order of dominance. Begin socialising with adults and children for short periods. Begins to become aware of its environment.
FOURTH	EIGHT TO TWELVE WEEKS	Brain is fully developed. Needs socialising with outside world. Remove from mother and littermates. Needs to change from canine pack to human pack. Human dominance necessary. Fear period occurs between 8 and 12 weeks. Avoid fright and pain.
FIFTH	THIRTEEN TO SIXTEEN WEEKS	Training and formal obedience should begin. Less association with other dogs, more with people, places, situations. Period will pass easily if you remember this is pup's change-to-adolescence time. Be firm and fair. Flight instinct prominent. Permissiveness and over-disciplining can do permanent damage. Praise for good behaviour.
JUVENILE	FOUR TO EIGHT MONTHS	Another fear period about 7 to 8 months of age. It passes quickly, but be cautious of fright and pain. Sexual maturity reached. Dominant traits established. Dog should understand sit, down, come and stay by now.

NOTE: THESE ARE APPROXIMATE TIME FRAMES. ALLOW FOR INDIVIDUAL DIFFERENCES IN PUPPIES.

every hour for an eight-week-old, for example, and always immediately after eating or sleeping. There is a reflex called the gastro-colic reflex (stomach-large bowel reflex). This means that after the stomach is stimulated by food, the puppy's bowel needs to be active too; this reflex is found in human babies as well as in puppies. The older the puppy, the less often he will need to relieve himself, and as a mature healthy adult, he will require only three to five relief trips per day.

Housing

Since the types of housing and control you provide for your puppy have a direct relationship on the success of house-training, we consider the various aspects of both before we begin training.

Bringing a new puppy home and turning him loose in your house can be compared to turning a child loose in a sports arena and telling him that the place is all his! The sheer enormity of the place would be too much for him to handle.

Instead, offer the puppy clearly defined areas where he can play, sleep, eat and live. A room of the house where the family gathers is the most popular choice. Puppies are social animals and need to feel a part of the pack right from the start. Hearing your voice, watching you while you are doing things and smelling you

nearby are all positive reinforcers that he is now a member of your pack. Usually a family room, the kitchen or a nearby adjoining breakfast area is ideal for providing safety and security for both puppy and owner.

Within that room there should be a smaller area that the puppy can call his own. An alcove or fenced (not boarded!) corner from which he can view the activities of his new family will be fine. The size of the area is the key factor here. It must be large enough for the puppy to lie down and stretch out as well as stand up, yet small enough so that he cannot relieve himself at one end and sleep at the other without coming into contact with his droppings before he is fully trained to relieve himself outside. Remember, it will not be long before the little puppy becomes a gangly adolescent and then a large adult.

The designated area should be lined with clean bedding and a toy. Water must always be available, in a non-spill container, once house training has been achieved.

Control

By control, we mean helping the puppy to create a lifestyle pattern that will be compatible to that of his human pack (YOU!). Just as we guide little children to learn our way of life, we must show the puppy when it is time to play, eat,

HOW MANY TIMES A DAY?

AGE	RELIEF TRIPS
To 14 weeks	10
14–22 weeks	8
22–32 weeks	6
Adulthood	4
(dog stops growing)	

These are estimates, of course, but they are a guide to the MINIMUM opportunities a dog should have each day to relieve himself.

sleep, exercise and even entertain himself.

Your puppy should always sleep in his bed. He should also learn that, during times of household confusion and excessive human activity such as at breakfast when family members are preparing for the day, he can play by himself in relative safety and comfort in his designated area. Each time you leave the puppy alone, he should understand exactly where he is to stay. You can gradually increase the time he is left alone to get him used to it.

Puppies are chewers. They cannot tell the difference between lamp cords, television wires, shoes, table legs, etc. Chewing into a television wire, for example, can be fatal to the puppy, while a shorted wire can start a fire in the house. If the puppy chews on the arm of the chair when he is alone, you will probably discipline him angrily when you get home. Thus, he makes the association that your coming home means he is going to be punished. (He will not remember chewing the chair and is incapable of making the association of the discipline with his naughty deed.)

Other times of excitement, such as family parties, etc. can be fun for the puppy, providing that he can view the activities from the security of his designated area. He is not underfoot and he is not being fed all sorts of titbits that will probably cause him stomach distress, yet he still feels a part of the fun.

SCHEDULE

A puppy should be taken to his relief area each time he is released from his designated area, after meals, after a play session and when he first awakens in the morning (at age eight weeks, this can mean 5 a.m.!). The puppy will indicate that he's ready 'to go' by circling or sniffing busily—do not misinterpret these signs. For a puppy less than ten weeks of age, a routine of taking him out every hour is necessary. As the puppy

Breeders commonly train puppies to newspapers, though this is not advisable with a large-breed dog. Unless completely impossible, train the Briard pup to the outdoors from the beginning.

grows, he will be able to wait for longer periods of time.

Keep trips to his relief area short. Stay no more than five or six minutes and then return to the house. If he goes during that time, praise him lavishly and take him indoors immediately. If does not, but he has an accident when you go back indoors, pick him up immediately, say 'No! No!' and return to his relief area. Wait a few minutes, and then return to

THE SUCCESS METHOD

6 Steps to Successful House-Training

1 Tell the puppy 'Nap time!' and place him in his special area with a small treat (a piece of cheese or half of a biscuit). Let him stay in the special area for five minutes while you are in the same room. Then release him and praise lavishly. Never release him when he is fussing. Wait until he is quiet before you let him out.

2 Repeat Step 1 several times a day.

3 The next day, place the puppy in the special area as before. Let him stay there for ten minutes. Do this several times.

4 Continue building time in five-minute increments until the puppy stays in his special area for 30 minutes with you in the room. Always take him to his relief area after prolonged periods in his special area.

5 Now go back to Step 1 and let the puppy stay in his special area for five minutes, this time while you are out of the room.

6 Once again, build time in the special area in five-minute increments with you out of the room. When the puppy will stay willingly in his special area (he may even fall asleep!) for 30 minutes with you out of the room, he will be ready to stay in it for several hours at a time.

the house again. Never hit a puppy or rub his face in urine or excrement when he has an accident.

Once indoors, put the puppy in his area until you have had time to clean up his accident. Then release him to the family area and watch him more closely than before. Chances are, his accident was a result of your not picking up his signal or waiting too long before offering him the opportunity to relieve himself. Never hold a grudge against the puppy for accidents.

Let the puppy learn that going outdoors means it is time to relieve himself, not play. Once trained, he will be able to play indoors and out and still differentiate between the times for play versus the times for relief.

Help him develop regular hours for naps, being alone, playing by himself and just resting, all in his bed. Encourage him to entertain himself while you are busy with your activities. Let him learn that having you near is comforting, but it is not you main purpose in life to provide him with undivided attention.

Each time you put a puppy in his own area, use the same command, whatever suits best. Soon, he will run to his bed or special area when he hears you say those words. Training a pup to his own designated area provides

safety for you, the puppy and the home. It also provides the puppy with a feeling of security, and that helps the puppy achieve self-confidence and clean habits.

Remember that one of the primary ingredients in house-training your puppy is control. Regardless of your lifestyle, there will always be occasions when you will need to have a place

KEY TO SUCCESS

Success that comes by luck is usually short-lived. Success that comes by well-thought-out proven methods is often more easily achieved and permanent. This is the Success Method. It is designed to give you, the puppy owner, a simple yet proven way to help your puppy develop clean living habits and a feeling of security in his new environment.

where your dog can stay and can be happy and safe. This method of training is the answer for now and in the future.

In conclusion, a few key elements are really all you need for a successful house-training method—consistency, frequency, praise, control and supervision. By following these procedures with a normal, healthy puppy, you and the puppy will soon be past the stage of 'accidents' and ready to move on to a full and rewarding life together.

RULES FOR GROUP LIVING

Both humans and dogs were designed to live in communities. If this had not been so, the dog would not have become part of human existence so easily. The African Wild Dog, more of a hyena than a dog, also lives in packs with important social relationships between pack members, but did not become integrated into the human world because its main method of social interaction was the regurgitation of stomach contents. If you liked the pack member who offered you this 'wonderful treat,' you ate it. This is not a viable starting point for interspecies interaction when one of the species is human.

Both humans and dogs have ranking systems within their communities. There are the pack leaders and there are the pack members, which are not as socially elevated. For either species' way of life, there have to be rules so that communal living is possible. In a wild dog community, a lot of time and energy would be wasted if each day someone threatened the pack leader to take over this position. Thus, the rules minimise the amount of energy spent on what are really quite counterproductive activities, and maximise the energy available for the useful activities of obtaining food and rearing babies.

Without these rules, chaos would reign supreme and the group would eventually perish. Humans and animals need some form of interspecies discipline in order to function effectively together as an extended type of pack. The most important rule for

PLAN TO PLAY

The puppy should have regular play and exercise sessions when he is with you or a family member. Exercise for a very young puppy can consist of a short walk around the house or garden. Exercise must not be much greater than this for most of the Briard's puppyhood, so that none of the growing bones or joints is harmed. Playing can include games with a special raggy, which will be helpful to chew during teething, but the dog's bite can be damaged by vigorous tug-of-war games.

your Briard is that he must learn where he is in the pack order, and that is ranking lower than each human family member. Once this hierarchy is in place, along with the benefits of further training, family life will be better for all.

A large humane society in an highly populated area recently surveyed dog owners regarding their satisfaction with their relationships with their dogs. People who had trained their dogs were 75% more satisfied with their pets than those who had never trained their dogs.

Psychologists have found that a behaviour pattern that results in something pleasant is likely to be repeated. One that results in something unpleasant is less likely to happen again. This is one of the theories upon which present-day training techniques are based. The idea is to manipulate the dog into doing something that you want him to do. Once he does this, you make sure that he realises that you are absolutely delighted, and the reward for this behaviour pattern will make him more likely to do it again because he enjoyed the end result.

Punishment is a subject that has many different things written about it. The latest ideas in dog behaviour studies consider it to be potentially more harmful than it was considered 20 years ago. Punishment takes the form of 'negative reinforcement,' such as

TRAINING TIP
Dogs will do anything for your attention. If you reward the dog when he is calm and resting, you will develop a well-mannered dog. If, on the other hand, you greet your dog excitedly and encourage him to wrestle with you, the dog will greet you the same way and you will have a hyperactive dog on your hands.

shouting at the dog, or the withdrawal of something positive, such as taking a toy or food away.

The effect of punishment can never be foreseen. Experiments have shown that it can lead to fight, fear, helplessness, avoidance or flight. Some believe that its effects are not long-lasting, even if it was effective as a 'quick fix' at the time. It is believed that punishment has little to do with learning as it does not change the motivation to perform a certain behaviour, but only prevents the behaviour from occurring while the punishment is carried out. The effect of punishment is based on fear, so it can be a dangerous method of modifying behaviour.

The effect of punishment depends both on the breed and on the individual dog. The Briard is less distressed by being scolded than a more sensitive breed such as one of the sighthounds would be, but is more greatly affected than a breed like the Labrador Retriever, which can seem not to register fully that you are unhappy with its behaviour.

There may be the case of the dog's getting rewards from its undesirable behaviour, so either the reward must be removed or the dog must be diverted into doing something that deserves a reward. A dog that jumps to get attention can be told to stand instead for the same attention. The dog that guards its food bowl from you can learn instead that your approach means that he will get small food rewards for good behaviour. Diverting the barking dog's attention provides a brief period of silence that can be rewarded.

A more difficult circumstance is with the dog that chases a jogger or a car and feels rewarded when what he is chasing goes away, just as he wanted.

Regardless of what the specific behaviour problem is, it is important to evaluate the situation to determine if some situational reward is involved.

TRAINING EQUIPMENT

COLLAR AND LEAD
For a Briard, the collar and lead that you use for training must be one with which you are easily

PICKING UP SIGNALS
Dogs are experts at non-verbal language. For example, when you arrive somewhere, you may not feel that you are signalling this to your dog, but often the dog manages to pick up signals and demonstrates that he realises that you are at the journey's end.

Dogs react to human speech, but for them it is a series of noises rather than words, with some events associated with some of the noises. If you say 'No, Oliver' in a very soft pleasant voice, it will not have the same meaning as 'No, Oliver!!' when you shout it as loudly as you can. You should never use the dog's name during a reprimand, just the command NO!!

Since dogs do not understand the actual words, comics can train them to respond in a way that is the opposite of the command given; for example, standing up at the command 'sit.'

able to work, not too heavy for the dog and perfectly safe.

TREATS

Have a bag of treats on hand; unfortunately, it seems that the messier the treat, the better it works! A soft treat such as cheese, liver or a piece of cooked chicken will be more successful than a dry biscuit, because it is thought that by the time the dog has finished chewing a dry treat, he will have forgotten why he is being rewarded in the first place. Using food rewards will not teach a dog to beg at table, the only way to teach a dog to beg at table is to give him food from the table. In training, rewarding the dog with a food treat will help him associate praise and the treats with learning new behaviours that obviously please his owner.

TRAINING BEGINS: ASK THE DOG A QUESTION

In order to teach your dog anything, you must first get his attention. After all, he cannot learn anything if he is looking away from you with his mind on something else. To get his attention, ask him 'School?' and immediately walk over to him and give him a treat as you tell him 'Good dog.' Wait a minute or two and repeat the routine, this time with a treat in your hand as you approach within 30 cms of the dog. Do not go directly to him, but

stop about 30 cms short of him and hold out the treat as you ask, 'School?' He will see you approaching with a treat in your hand and most likely begin walking toward you. As you meet, give him the treat and praise again.

The third time, ask the question, have a treat in your hand and walk only a short distance toward the dog so that he must walk almost all the way to you. As he reaches you, give him the treat and praise again.

By this time, the dog will probably be getting the idea that if he pays attention to you, especially when you ask that question, it will pay off in treats and enjoyable activities for him.

Remember that the dog does not understand your verbal language, he only recognises sounds. Your question translates into a series of sounds for him, and those sounds become the signal to go to you and pay attention; if he does, he will get to interact with you plus receive treats and praise.

THE BASIC COMMANDS

TEACHING SIT

Now that you have the dog's attention, attach his lead and hold it in your left hand and a food treat in your right. Place your food hand at the dog's nose and let him lick the treat but not take it from

Most trainers begin with the sit command because it is generally the easiest for dogs to learn. Once success is met with the first command, the subsequent commands become easier.

you. Say 'sit' and slowly raise your food hand from in front of the dog's nose up over his head so that he is looking at the ceiling. As he bends his head upward, he will have to bend his knees to maintain his balance. As he bends his knees, he will assume a sit position. At that point, release the food treat and praise lavishly with comments such as 'Good dog! Good sit!', etc. Remember to always praise enthusiastically, because dogs relish verbal praise from their owners and feel so proud of themselves whenever they accomplish a behaviour pattern of which their owners approve.

You will not use food forever in getting the dog to obey your commands. Food is only used to teach new behaviours, and once the dog knows what you want

when you give a specific command, you will wean him off the food treats but still maintain the verbal praise. After all, you will always have your voice with you, and there will be many times when you have no food rewards but expect the dog to obey.

TEACHING DOWN

Teaching the down exercise is easy when you understand how the dog perceives the down position, and it is very difficult when you do not. Dogs perceive the down position as a submissive one; therefore, teaching the down exercise using a forceful method can sometimes make the dog develop such a fear of the down that he either runs away when

TRAINING CLUBS

The Kennel Club will have the addresses of the training clubs near you. For a token amount of money, you will get advice from people interested in training dogs, sometimes from people with professional training qualifications. Dog and owner attend the sessions once a week, but you also have to practise in short sessions, several times each day, at home. If this is done properly, the whole procedure will result in a well-mannered dog and an owner who delights in living with a pet that is eager to please and enjoys doing things with his owner.

DOUBLE JEOPARDY
A dog in jeopardy never lies down. He stays alert on his feet because instinct tells him that he may have to run away or fight for his survival. Therefore, if a dog feels threatened or anxious, he will not lie down. Consequently, it is important to have the dog calm and relaxed as he learns the down exercise.

you say 'Down' or attempts to snap at the person who tries to force him down.

Have the dog sit close alongside your left leg, facing in the same direction as you are. Hold the lead in your left hand and a food treat in your right. Now place your left hand lightly on the top of the dog's shoulders where they meet above the spinal cord. Do not push down on the dog's shoulders; simply rest your left hand there so you can guide the dog to lie down close to your left leg rather than to swing away from your side when he drops.

Now place the food hand at the dog's nose, say 'Down' very softly (almost a whisper), and slowly lower the food hand to the dog's front feet. When the food hand reaches the floor, begin moving it forward along the floor in front of the dog. Keep talking softly to the dog, saying things like, 'Do you want this treat? You can do this, good dog.' Your

reassuring tone of voice will help calm the dog as he tries to follow the food hand in order to get the treat.

When the dog's elbows touch the floor, release the food and praise softly. Try to get the dog to maintain that down position for several seconds before you let him sit up again. The goal here is to get the dog to settle down and not to feel threatened in the down position.

TEACHING STAY

It is easy to teach most dogs to stay in either a sit or down position. Again we use food and praise during the teaching process as we help the dog to understand exactly what it is we are expecting him to do.

To teach the sit/stay, start with the dog sitting on your left side and hold the lead in your left hand. Have a food treat in your right hand and place your food

Never use a forceful method to teach the down command. Once the Briard realises that he is not being threatened in the down position, he will assume it without too much fuss.

hand at the dog's nose. Stay 'Stay' and step out on your right foot to stand directly in front of the dog, toe to toe, as he licks and nibbles the treat. Be sure to keep his head facing upwards to maintain the sit position. Count to five and then swing around to stand next to your dog again with him on your left. As soon as you get back to the original position, release the food and praise lavishly.

To teach the down/stay, do the down as previously described. As soon as the dog lies down, say 'Stay' and step out on your right foot just as you did in the sit/stay. Count to five and then return to stand beside the dog with him on your left side. Release the treat, and praise as always.

Within a week or ten days you can begin to add a bit of distance between you and your dog when you leave him. When you do, use your left hand open with the palm facing the dog as a stay signal, much the same as the hand signal a constable uses to stop traffic at a junction. Hold the food treat in your right hand as before, but this time the food is not touching the dog's nose. He will watch the food hand and quickly learn that he is going to get that treat as soon as you return to his side.

When you can stand one metre away from your dog for 30 seconds, then you can begin building time and distance in both stays. Eventually, the dog

can be expected to remain in the stay position for prolonged periods of time until you return to him or call him to you. Always praise lavishly when he stays.

Practise the stay command in both the sit and down position. In time you can build up time and distance between you and the Briard.

come when called. The secret, it seems, is never to teach the word 'come.'

At times when an owner most wants his dog to come when called, the owner is likely upset or anxious and he allows these feelings to come through in the tone of his voice when he calls his dog. Hearing that desperation in his owner's voice, the dog fears the results of going to him and therefore either disobeys outright

TEACHING COME

If you make teaching 'come' an enjoyable experience, you should never have a 'student' that does not love the game or that fails to

'COME' . . . BACK

Never call your dog to come to you for a correction or scold him when he reaches you. That is the quickest way to turn a 'Come' command into 'Go away fast!' Dogs think only in the present tense, and your dog will connect the scolding with coming to you, not with his misbehaviour of a few moments earlier.

or runs in the opposite direction. The secret, therefore, is to teach the dog a game and, when you want him to come you, simply play the game. It is practically a no-fail solution!

To begin, have several members of your family take a few food treats and each go into a different room in the house. Take turns calling the dog, and each person should celebrate the dog's finding him with a treat and lots of happy praise. When a person

Training the
Briard to heel at
the owner's side
is essential for a
dog as powerful
as this. Begin
training the
puppy to heel,
and practise with
the dog through-
out his life.

followed by 'Where are you?' For example, a woman has a 12-year-old companion dog who went blind, but who never fails to locate her owner when asked, 'Where are you?'

Children particularly love to play this game with their dogs. Children can hide in smaller places like a shower or bath, behind a bed or under a table. The dog needs to work a little bit harder to find these hiding places, but when he does, he loves to celebrate with a treat and a gentle tussle with a favourite youngster.

calls the dog, he is actually inviting the dog to find him and get a treat as a reward for 'winning.'

A few turns of the 'Where are you?' game and the dog will understand that everyone is playing the game and that each person has a big celebration awaiting the dog's success at locating him. Once he learns to love the game, simply calling out 'Where are you?' will bring the dog running from wherever he is when he hears that all-important question.

The come command is recognised as one of the most important things to teach a dog, but there are trainers who work with thousands of dogs and never teach the actual word 'come'. Yet these dogs will race to respond to a person who uses the dog's name

TEACHING HEEL

Heeling means that the dog walks beside the owner without pulling. It takes time and patience on the owner's part to succeed at teaching the dog that he (the owner) will not proceed unless the dog is walking calmly beside him. Pulling out ahead on the lead is definitely not acceptable.

Begin with holding the lead in your left hand as the dog sits beside your left leg. Move the loop end of the lead to your right hand but keep your left hand short on the lead so it keeps the dog close next to you.

Say 'Heel' and step forward on your left foot. Keep the dog close to you and take three steps. Stop and have the dog sit next to you in what we now call the 'heel position.' Praise verbally, but do not touch the dog. Hesitate a moment and begin again with 'Heel,' taking three steps and stopping, at which point the dog is told to sit again.

Your goal here is to have the dog walk those three steps without pulling on the lead. When he will walk calmly beside you for three steps without pulling, increase the number of steps you take to five. When he will walk politely beside you while you take five steps, you can increase the length of your walk to ten steps. Keep increasing the length of your stroll until the dog will walk quietly beside you without pulling as long as you want him to heel. When you stop heeling, indicate to the dog that the exercise is over by verbally praising as you pet him and say 'OK, good dog.' The 'OK' is used as a release word, meaning that the exercise is finished and the dog is free to relax.

If you are dealing with a dog who insists on pulling you around, simply 'put on your brakes' and stand your ground until the dog realises that the two of you are not going anywhere until he is beside you and moving at your pace not his. It may take some time just standing there to convince the dog that you are the leader and you will be the one to decide on the direction and speed of your travel.

Each time the dog looks up at you or slows down to give a slack lead between the two of you, quietly praise him and say, 'Good

FEAR AGGRESSION

Pups who are subjected to physical abuse during training commonly end up with behavioural problems as adults. One common result of abuse is fear aggression, in which a dog will lash out, bare his teeth, snarl and finally bite someone by whom he feels threatened. For example, your daughter may be playing with the dog one afternoon. As they play hide-and-seek, she backs the dog into a corner and, as she attempts to tease him playfully, he bites her hand. Examine the cause of this behaviour. Did your daughter ever hit the dog? Did someone who resembles your daughter hit or scream at the dog?

Fortunately, fear aggression is relatively easy to correct. Have your daughter engage in only positive activities with the dog, such as feeding, petting and walking. She should not give any corrections or negative feedback. If the dog still growls or cowers away from her, allow someone else to accompany them. After approximately one week, the dog should feel that he can rely on her for many positive things, and he will also be prevented from reacting fearfully towards anyone who might resemble her.

Heel training is
the first step for
show dogs to
learn how to gait
properly in the
ring, without
pulling ahead of
the handler or
running out of
control.

food treats. At first, give a treat after each exercise. Then, start to give a treat only after every other exercise. Mix up the times when you offer a food reward and the times when you only offer praise so that the dog will never know when he is going to receive both food and praise and when he is going to receive only praise. This is called a variable ratio reward system and it proves successful because there is always the chance that the owner will produce a treat, so the dog never stops trying for the reward. No matter what, *always* give verbal praise.

OBEDIENCE CLASSES

It is a good idea to enrol in an obedience class if one is available in your area. If yours is a show dog, ringcraft classes would be more appropriate. Many areas have dog clubs that offer basic obedience training as well as preparatory classes for obedience competition. There are also local

heel. Good dog.' Eventually, the dog will begin to respond and within a few days he will be walking politely beside you without pulling the lead. At first, the training sessions should be kept short and very positive; soon the dog will be able to walk nicely with you for increasingly longer distances. Remember also to give the dog free time and the opportunity to run and play when you are done with heel practice.

WEANING OFF FOOD IN TRAINING

Food is used in training new behaviours. Once the dog understands what behaviour goes with a specific command, it is time to start weaning him off the

TUG OF WALK?
If you begin teaching the heel by taking long walks and letting the dog pull you along, he misinterprets this action as an acceptable form of taking a walk. When you pull back on the lead to counteract his pulling, he reads that tug as a signal to pull even harder!

KEEP AN OPEN MIND

Dogs are as different from each other as people are. What works for one dog may not work for another. Have an open mind. If one method of training is unsuccessful, try another.

dog trainers who offer similar classes. Phoning The Kennel Club will give you a contact number for your local training and ringcraft clubs.

At obedience shows, dogs can earn titles at various levels of competition. The beginning levels of competition include basic behaviours such as sit, down, heel, etc. The more advanced levels of competition include retrieving, scent discrimination and signal work. The advanced levels require a dog and owner to put a lot of time and effort into their training, and the titles that can be earned at these levels of competition are very prestigious.

The highest level of obedience in Britain is Championship Class C. At Obedience Championship Shows, an Obedience Certificate is awarded to the winner of Class C for dogs, and another to the winner of Class C for bitches, provided that neither has lost more than 15 points out of a total of 300 for the exercises carried out. When a dog or bitch has three of these certificates, he or she gains the title of Obedience Champion.

At Crufts each year, all the previous year's Certificate winners compete for The Kennel Club Obedience Championship. These awards started just after the Second World War, when they were dominated by German Shepherd Dogs. More recently the Border Collie and its close relation, the working sheepdog, have been the main winners of these high awards, though a few other breeds produce the occasional top-quality obedience dog (Golden Retriever, Dobermann). Perhaps it will not be long until a Briard manages to get to these dizzying heights; with a lot of work, the Briard would be capable.

In the United States, a much greater number of dogs win obedience titles because the requirements are much less stringent.

The long jump is easily cleared by this Briard, competing in an obedience show.

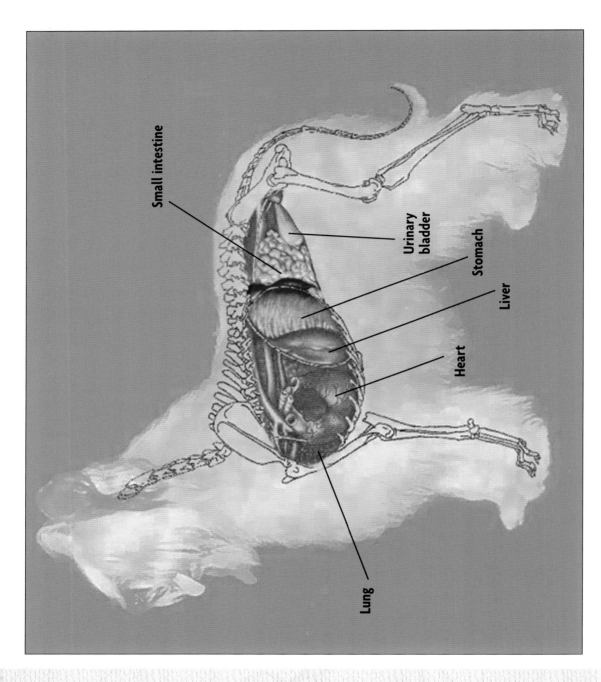

Small intestine

Urinary bladder

Stomach

Liver

Heart

Lung

INTERNAL STRUCTURE OF THE BRIARD

Dogs suffer from many of the same physical illnesses as people. They might even share many of the same psychological problems. Since people usually know more about human diseases than canine maladies, many of the terms used in this chapter will be familiar but not necessarily those used by veterinary surgeons. We use the term *x-rays* instead of *radiographs.* We will also use the familiar term *symptoms* even though dogs don't have symptoms, which are verbal descriptions of something the patient feels or observes himself, which he regards as abnormal. Dogs have *clinical signs*, since they cannot speak, so we have to look for these clinical signs...but we still use the term *symptoms* in the book.

Medicine is a constantly changing art, with some scientific input as well. Things alter as we learn more and more about basic sciences such as genetics and biochemistry, and have use of more sophisticated imaging techniques such as Computer Aided Tomography (CAT scans) or Magnetic Resonance Imaging (MRI scans). There is academic dispute about many canine maladies, and different veterinary surgeons treat them in different ways. Some vets have a greater emphasis on surgical techniques than others.

SELECTING A VETERINARY SURGEON

Your selection of a veterinary surgeon should be based on personal recommendation for his skills with small animals, especially dogs. If the vet is based nearby, it will be helpful because you might have an emergency or need to make multiple visits for treatments.

All veterinary surgeons are licenced, and in Britain are Members of the Royal College of Veterinary Surgeons (MRCVS after their names). The high street veterinary practice deals with routine medical problems such as infections, injuries and the promotion of health, for example, by vaccination. If the problem affecting your dog is more complex, in Britain your vet will refer your pet to someone with a more detailed knowledge of the problem. This will usually be a specialist at the nearest university veterinary school who is a veterinary dermatologist, veterinary ophthalmologist, etc.

Veterinary procedures are very costly and as the treatments available improve, they are going to become more expensive. It is quite acceptable to discuss matters of cost with your vet; if there is more than one treatment option, cost may be a factor in deciding which route to take.

Insurance against veterinary cost is also becoming very popular. This will not pay for routine vaccinations but will cover the costs for unexpected emergencies such as emergency surgery after a road traffic accident.

PREVENTATIVE MEDICINE

It is much easier, less costly and more effective to practise preventative medicine than to fight bouts of illness and disease. Properly bred puppies from all breeds come from parents that were selected based upon their genetic disease profile. Luckily, the Briard is much less affected by genetic disease than many other, more popular, breeds.

The puppies' mothers should have been vaccinated, free of all internal and external parasites, and properly nourished. For these reasons, a visit to the veterinary surgeon who cared for the dam (mother) is recommended, if at all possible. The dam passes disease resistance to her puppies, which should last from eight to ten weeks. Unfortunately, she can also pass on parasites and infection. This is why knowledge about her health is useful in learning more about the health of the puppies.

WEANING TO FIVE MONTHS OLD

Puppies should be weaned by the time they are two months old. A puppy that remains for at least eight weeks with its mother and littermates usually adapts better to other dogs and people later in its life.

Some new owners have their puppy examined by a veterinary surgeon immediately, which is a good idea unless the puppy is overtired by a long journey. Vaccination programmes usually begin when the puppy is very young.

The puppy will have its teeth examined and have its skeletal conformation and general health checked prior to certification by the veterinary surgeon. Puppies in certain breeds have problems with their kneecaps, cataracts and other eye problems, heart murmurs and undescended testicles. They may also have personality problems and your veterinary surgeon might have training in temperament evaluation.

VACCINATION SCHEDULING

Most vaccinations are given by injection and should only be given by a veterinary surgeon. Both he and you should keep a record of the date of the injection,

HEALTH AND VACCINATION SCHEDULE

AGE IN WEEKS:	6TH	8TH	10TH	12TH	14TH	16TH	20-24TH	52ND
Worm Control	✔	✔	✔	✔	✔	✔	✔	
Neutering								✔
Heartworm		✔		✔		✔	✔	
Parvovirus	✔		✔		✔		✔	✔
Distemper		✔		✔		✔		✔
Hepatitis		✔		✔		✔		✔
Leptospirosis								✔
Parainfluenza	✔		✔		✔			✔
Dental Examination		✔					✔	✔
Complete Physical		✔					✔	✔
Coronavirus				✔			✔	✔
Kennel Cough	✔							
Hip Dysplasia								✔
Rabies							✔	

Vaccinations are not instantly effective. It takes about two weeks for the dog's immune system to develop antibodies. Most vaccinations require annual booster shots. Your veterinary surgeon should guide you in this regard.

the identification of the vaccine and the amount given. Some vets give a first vaccination at eight weeks, but most dog breeders prefer the course not to commence until about 10 weeks because of interaction with the antibodies produced by the mother. The vaccination scheduling is usually based on a 15-day cycle. You must take your vet's advice as to when to vaccinate, as this may differ according to the vaccine used. The usual vaccines contain immunising doses of several different viruses, such as distemper, parvovirus, parainfluenza and hepatitis. There are other vaccines available when the puppy is at risk. You should rely upon professional advice. This is especially true for the booster immunisations. Most vaccination programmes require a booster when the puppy is a year old and once a year thereafter. In some cases, circumstances may require more frequent immunisations.

Kennel cough, more formally known as tracheobronchitis, is immunised against with a vaccine that is sprayed into the dog's nostrils. Kennel cough is usually

KNOWING YOUR VETERINARY SURGEON

By the time your dog is a year old, you should have become very comfortable with your local veterinary surgeon and have agreed on scheduled visits for booster vaccinations. The eyes, ears, nose and throat also should be examined regularly.

included in routine vaccination, but it is often not as effective as the vaccines for other major diseases.

FIVE MONTHS TO ONE YEAR OF AGE

Unless you intend to breed from or show your dog, the general advice is to get your dog neutered. By the time your Briard is seven or eight months of age, it is possible to have some idea how closely he will adhere to the standard of the breed, although he still has a lot of growing to do. If there are any serious faults, they will be obvious, although it is still easy to ruin a promising puppy of this age with inadvisable feeding and exercise. If your Briard grows up to be a less-than-average specimen, not only will you win little, and any wins you do have will be to the detriment of the breed, but he also should not be used to breed from.

DOGS OLDER THAN ONE YEAR

Continue to visit the veterinary surgeon at least once a year. There is no such disease as 'old age,' but bodily functions do change with age. The eyes and ears are no longer as efficient. Liver, kidney and intestinal functions often decline. Proper dietary changes, recommended by your veterinary surgeon, can make life more pleasant for your ageing Briard and you.

SKIN PROBLEMS IN THE BRIARD

Veterinary surgeons are consulted by dog owners for skin problems more than any other group of diseases or maladies. Dog's skin is as sensitive, if not more so, than human skin and both suffer almost the same ailments (though the occurrence of acne in dogs is rare!). For this reason, veterinary dermatology has developed into a speciality practiced by many veterinary surgeons.

Since many skin problems have visual symptoms that are almost identical, it requires the skill of an experienced veterinary dermatologist to identify and cure many of the more severe skin disorders. Pet shops sell many treatments for skin problems but most of the treatments are directed at symptoms and not at the underlying problem(s). If your dog is suffering from a skin disorder, you should seek professional assistance as quickly as possible. As with all diseases, the earlier a problem is identified and treated, the more successful can be the treatment.

PARASITE BITES

Many of us are allergic to insect bites. The bites itch, erupt and may even become infected. Dogs have the same reaction to fleas, ticks and/or mites. When an insect lands on you, you have the chance to whisk it away with your hand. Unfortunately, when a dog is bitten by a flea, tick or mite, it

can only scratch it away or bite it. By the time the dog has been bitten, the parasite has done some of its damage. It may also have laid eggs, which will cause further problems in the near future. The itching from parasite bites is probably due to the saliva injected into the site when the parasite sucks the dog's blood.

AIRBORNE ALLERGIES

An interesting allergy is pollen allergy. Humans have hay fever from which they suffer during the pollinating season. Many dogs

DISEASE REFERENCE CHART

	What is it?	What causes it?	Symptoms
Leptospirosis	Severe disease that affects the internal organs; can be spread to people.	A bacterium, which is often carried by rodents, that enters through mucous membranes and spreads quickly throughout the body.	Range from fever, vomiting and loss of appetite in less severe cases to shock, irreversible kidney damage and possibly death in most severe cases.
Rabies	Potentially deadly virus that infects warm-blooded mammals. Not seen in United Kingdom.	Bite from a carrier of the virus, mainly wild animals.	1st stage: dog exhibits change in behaviour, fear. 2nd stage: dog's behaviour becomes more aggressive. 3rd stage: loss of coordination, trouble with bodily functions.
Parvovirus	Highly contagious virus, potentially deadly.	Ingestion of the virus, which is usually spread through the faeces of infected dogs.	Most common: severe diarrhoea. Also vomiting, fatigue, lack of appetite.
Kennel cough	Contagious respiratory infection.	Combination of types of bacteria and virus. Most common: *Bordetella bronchiseptica* bacteria and parainfluenza virus.	Chronic cough.
Distemper	Disease primarily affecting respiratory and nervous system.	Virus that is related to the human measles virus.	Mild symptoms such as fever, lack of appetite and mucous secretion progress to evidence of brain damage, 'hard pad.'
Hepatitis	Virus primarily affecting the liver.	Canine adenovirus type I (CAV-1). Enters system when dog breathes in particles.	Lesser symptoms include listlessness, diarrhoea, vomiting. More severe symptoms include 'blue-eye' (clumps of virus in eye).
Coronavirus	Virus resulting in digestive problems.	Virus is spread through infected dog's faeces.	Stomach upset evidenced by lack of appetite, vomiting, diarrhoea.

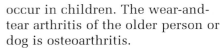

suffer from the same allergies. When the pollen count is high, your dog might suffer but don't expect him to sneeze and have a runny nose as a human would. Dogs react to pollen allergies in the same way they react to fleas—they scratch and bite themselves.

Dogs, like humans, can be tested for allergens. Discuss the testing with your veterinary surgeon.

Auto-Immune Skin Problems

Auto-immune illnesses are ones in which the immune system overacts and does not recognise parts of you, but starts to react as if these parts were foreign and need to be destroyed. For example, rheumatoid arthritis occurs when the body does not recognise the joints, and this leads to a very painful and damaging reaction in the joints that is nothing to do with age, so can

occur in children. The wear-and-tear arthritis of the older person or dog is osteoarthritis.

Lupus is an auto-immune disease that affects dogs as well as people. It can take variable forms, affecting the kidneys, bones and the skin. It can be fatal, so is treated with steroids, which can themselves have very significant side effects. The steroids calm down the allergic reaction to the body's tissues, which helps the lupus, but also calms down the body's reaction to real foreign substances such as bacteria, and also thins skin and bone.

FOOD PROBLEMS

Food Allergies

Dogs are allergic to many foods that are best-sellers and highly recommended by breeders and veterinary surgeons. Changing the brand of food that you buy may not eliminate the problem if the element to which the dog is allergic is contained in the new brand.

Recognising a food allergy can be difficult. Humans often have a rash when they eat a food to which they are allergic, or have swelling of the lips or eyes. Dogs do not usually develop a rash, but react in the same way as they would to an airborne or bite allergy—they itch, scratch and bite. While pollen allergies and parasite bites are usually seasonal,

DID YOU KNOW?

Not every breed of dog has similar ears. The Briard has lots of hair around the ears so that they are not really open to the air. The circulation of air helps to keep the ears healthy, so it is important to check your Briard's ears regularly. You should not probe inside your dog's ears as you may cause damage. Only clean the parts that are accessible with a soft cotton wipe.

food allergies are year 'round problems.

TREATING FOOD ALLERGY

Diagnosis of food allergy is based on a two-to-four-week dietary trial with a home-cooked diet fed to the exclusion of all other foods. The diet should consist of boiled rice or potato, with a source of protein that the dog has never eaten before, such as fresh or frozen fish, lamb or even something as exotic as pheasant. Water has to be the only drink, and it is really important that no other foods should be fed during this trial. If the dog's condition improves, you need to try the original diet once again to see if the itching starts again. If it does, then this confirms the diagnosis that the dog is allergic to its original diet. Treatment is to feed long-term on something that does not distress the dog's skin, which may be in the form of one of the commercially available hypoaller-genic diets or the home-made diet that you created for the allergy trial.

FOOD INTOLERANCE

Food intolerance is the inability of the dog to completely digest certain foods. This occurs because the dog does not have the chemicals necessary to digest some foodstuffs. These chemicals are called enzymes. All puppies have the enzymes necessary to digest canine milk, but some dogs do not have the enzymes to digest a very different form of milk that is commonly found in human households: milk from cows. In this case, drinking cows' milk gives them loose bowels, stomach pains and the passage of gas. The Briard's stomach can be a very delicate organ, so be careful about any foodstuffs that are causing distress. Dogs often do not have the enzymes to digest Soya or other beans. Treatment means excluding the foodstuffs that upset your Briard's digestion.

BLOAT OR GASTRIC TORSION

Bloat is a terrible killer of the young, otherwise healthy, adult or the more elderly dog. It is a problem found in the large, deep-

FEEDING TIP

Feeding your dog correctly is very important. You are what you eat; this holds true for dogs as well as humans. An incorrect diet affects health and behaviour. Its most visible effect is to the skin and coat, but all internal organs are affected similarly.

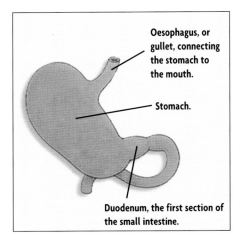

Oesophagus, or gullet, connecting the stomach to the mouth.

Stomach.

Duodenum, the first section of the small intestine.

chested breeds, and is the subject of much research, but still manages to take away many dogs before their time in a very horrible way.

The diagram to the right, showing a cross-section through a Briard, shows how deep the body cavity is. The muscles drawn are those around the vertebrae that give strength to the back and allow it to be flexed and stretched when running.

The stomach hangs like a handbag with both straps broken within this deep body cavity. The above cross-section is similar to the cross-section of the body cavity, but it demonstrates another way that the stomach is held in place. There is the support provided by the junction with the oesophagus, or gullet, and there is the support provided by the junction with the first part of the small intestine, the broken straps

of the handbag. The only other support comes from a thin layer of partially opaque 'internal skin' called the peritoneum, illustrated on the facing page.

No wonder the stomach can move around easily, and those breeds with the deepest chests are at the greatest risk of the whole stomach's twisting round (gastric torsion), cutting off the blood supply and preventing the stomach contents from leaving, and increasing the amount of gas in the stomach.

Once these things have happened, surgery is vital. If the blood supply has been cut off too long and a bit of the stomach wall dies, death of the Briard is almost inevitable.

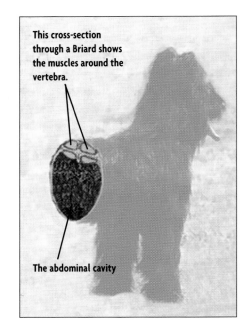

This cross-section through a Briard shows the muscles around the vertebra.

The abdominal cavity

The horrendous pain of this condition is due to the stomach wall's being stretched by the gas caught in the stomach, as well as the pain of the stomach wall's desperately needing the blood that cannot get to it. This is the pain of not being able to pass wind, not just a normal amount of wind but a huge amount, with a pain equivalent to that of an heart attack on top. This pain is due to the heart muscle's being starved of blood.

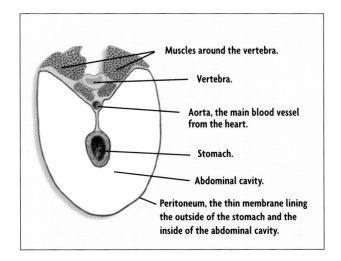

Muscles around the vertebra.

Vertebra.

Aorta, the main blood vessel from the heart.

Stomach.

Abdominal cavity.

Peritoneum, the thin membrane lining the outside of the stomach and the inside of the abdominal cavity.

TRY TO PREVENT BLOAT
- Wait for at least an hour after exercise to feed your Briard.
- Wait for at least an hour after feeding to exercise your Briard.
- Do not feed on cheap, high-cereal-content food;
- Feed on the high-protein, low-residue diets;
- Raise food and water bowls to try to reduce any air swallowed;
- If your Briard is greedy and eats quickly, reduce the air swallowed by putting something large and inedible in the bowl so he has to pick around it and to eat more slowly.

DETECTING BLOAT
- Your dog's stomach starts to distend, ending up large and as tight as a football;
- Your dog is dribbling, as no saliva can be swallowed;
- Your dog makes frequent attempts to vomit but, as the

stomach is closed off, it cannot bring anything up;
- Your dog is distressed from the pain;
- Your dog starts to suffer from clinical shock. This means that there is not enough blood in the dog's circulation as the hard, dilated stomach stops the blood from getting back to the heart to be pumped around. Clinical shock is seen by pale gums and tongue, as they have been starved of blood. The shocked dog also has glazed, staring eyes.

You have minutes, yes *minutes*, to get your dog into surgery. If you see any of these things at any time of the day or night, get to the vet's surgery immediately as that is where all the equipment is. Someone will have to phone and warn that you

BRIARD

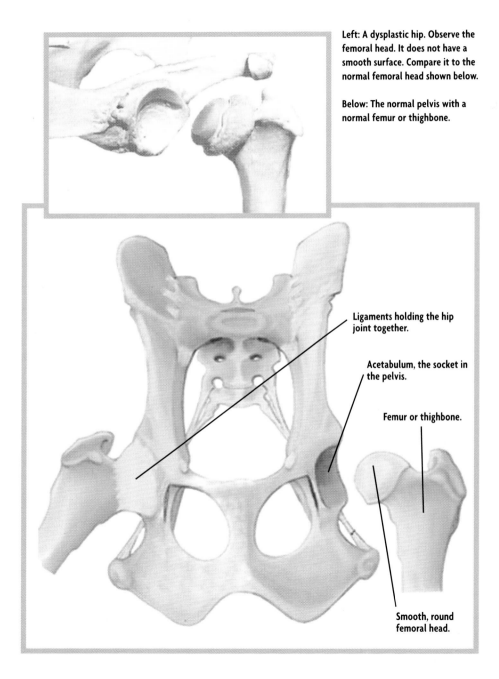

Left: A dysplastic hip. Observe the femoral head. It does not have a smooth surface. Compare it to the normal femoral head shown below.

Below: The normal pelvis with a normal femur or thighbone.

Ligaments holding the hip joint together.

Acetabulum, the socket in the pelvis.

Femur or thighbone.

Smooth, round femoral head.

are on your way so that they can be prepared to get your pet on the operating table—which is a great justification for having a mobile phone.

It is possible for a dog to have more than one incident of gastric torsion, even if it has had its stomach stapled to the inside of the chest wall to give extra support to prevent its twisting again.

HIP DYSPLASIA

This is a problem of the hip joint, when its two parts, the round end of the femur (thigh bone) and the round socket in the pelvis, do not fit together. In humans, all newborn babies are checked for this, and there are ways to try to help the growing joint develop in a more normal way. In dogs, it is not possible to detect it at birth, and often it is not picked up until the dog is an adult.

Briard colours are inherited as single genes, a Briard is either black or it is not. Hip dysplasia is inherited, but not as a single gene; many genes are involved in the creation of something as complex as a hip joint, and it is also believed that the environment in which the puppy grows up affects the way the joint develops.

The joint may be dysplastic (abnormally formed) if the femoral head is not completely round even though there is a normal socket, or there may be a nice round femoral head and the socket is too flattened to provide a tight fit. It may be abnormal for one or more reasons; when vets x-ray and examine the x-rays in detail for hip dysplasia, they look at nine different features.

Hip dysplasia is not a lethal condition, but it does cause a great deal of pain. The abnormal hip develops arthritis as the surfaces rub together in an abnormal way. Just consider the pain and lack of mobility of all the people on the waiting list for hip replacement... and very few of them were born with abnormal hips. The dog with hip dysplasia may have the same amount of arthritis as a dog several times its age, whose normal hips have suffered the wear-and-tear of old age. Hip replacement will help both dog and person, but this is an expensive operation, and not everyone can afford several thousand pounds for surgery for his dog.

The only way to diagnose hip dysplasia is by x-ray. The dog has to be anaesthetized so that it can be very still, lying on its back with its legs pulled down. The British scheme started in 1965, but the modern way of coding the x-rays started in 1978, initially with the German Shepherd Dog. This was because the leading expert on hip dysplasia, Dr Malcolm Willis, owned and bred the German Shepherd. He has continued to do a lot of work on the screening for hip dysplasia and other work on all of the genetic diseases of dogs.

A British hip dysplasia score comes in the form of two numbers, one for each hip and a total that is the sum of these two numbers. The x-rays are read by veterinary surgeons that hold the Diploma in Veterinary Radiology, a postgraduate few manage to attain. The worst possible score for one hip is 53 points; thus, if both hips are terrible, the score will be 53 + 53 = 106. A score of 0 is the best. In the Briard the average score is 22, which puts it as the eighth worst breed, and the range of scores was from 0 to 99.

Before buying a puppy, make sure that its parents have been hip scored, and have low scores, ideally less than 22. Because there is more than one gene involved in the inheritance of hip dysplasia, it is possible for your puppy to have hips that are much poorer than its parents. This is a reflection of the complexity of the situation, and how it is going to be a long-term process over many generations to eradicate this illness.

If you are unlucky enough to get a Briard with poor hips, the latest advice is to give short brisk walks that build up the muscles of the hindlegs, so as to keep the hip joint in as normal a position as possible. Surgery is the last option, and Dr Willis recommends a specialist surgeon.

EYE PROBLEMS IN THE BRIARD

RETINAL PIGMENT EPITHELIAL DYSTROPHY (RPED)

In Britain, The Kennel Club is involved with screening for hereditary eye disease as well as the hip dysplasia scheme. Professor Peter Bedford and his team are working on retinal pigment epithelial dystrophy, a condition that causes reduced vision in the Briard. This condition used to be called central progressive retinal atrophy before it was more fully understood.

What a lot of great long words! If we look at the anatomy of the eye, we can understand these words and the diseases they describe a little better.

The pigment epithelium is the first part of the retina that the light falls on. Both humans and Briards see things when the light falls on the next layer down, the rods and cones, and the message that light is coming in the eye goes off to the brain through the nerve cells. The pigment cells support the rods and cones, both physically and by providing them with oxygen and food in the form of the sugar glucose.

Retinal pigment epithelial dystrophy (RPED) means abnormality of the pigment cell layer of the retina. The retina is the light-sensitive 'skin' or epithelium at the back of the eye.

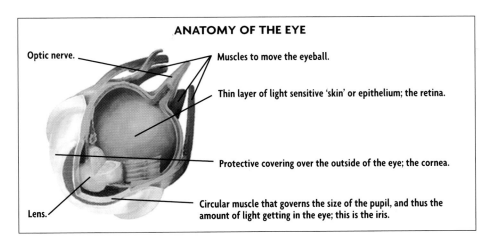

ANATOMY OF THE EYE

Optic nerve.

Muscles to move the eyeball.

Thin layer of light sensitive 'skin' or epithelium; the retina.

Protective covering over the outside of the eye; the cornea.

Lens.

Circular muscle that governs the size of the pupil, and thus the amount of light getting in the eye; this is the iris.

In RPED, the pigment cells do not work properly, and as a result the rods and cones die. As the light coming through the eye lands on dead rods and cones, the light energy cannot be transformed into electrical energy to go off to the brain, and so the dog cannot see anything in the area of the retina where the cells have died. In RPED, the rods and cones that die are the ones for vision immediately in front, leaving the dog with vision just around the edges.

RPED is a genetic illness that seems to be found more commonly in the Briards of Britain than the rest of the world. However, Professor Bedford feels that there are other factors at work as well. He and his team have discovered that the disease is most likely to be the result of a liver deficiency, which means that essential chemicals derived from vitamin E are not transported to the retina. Without these chemicals, the pigment cells cannot work properly and die. The liver deficiency is the inherited part of the illness, and

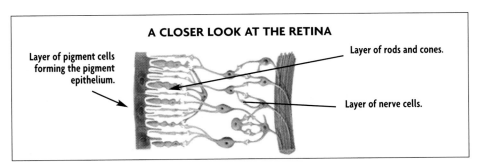

A CLOSER LOOK AT THE RETINA

Layer of pigment cells forming the pigment epithelium.

Layer of rods and cones.

Layer of nerve cells.

the only sign that a Briard has inherited RPED comes when parts of the retina start to die and the dog's vision is reduced.

The eye team also believes that that the amount of liver deficiency inherited is variable, and so the amount of retinal damage varies as well. The amount of vitamin E in the diet can also alter the amount of retinal damage the Briard suffers. If the dog is fed a diet rich in vitamin E, it can help the liver produce the chemical derivatives that the retina needs, reducing the severity of the retinal damage.

The eye-screening scheme has helped reduce the incidence of this illness. Regular eye checks have discovered the dogs with retinal damage, because it is relatively easy to look at the retina directly with the correct opththalmoscope if you have had the correct training (and the dog has had the correct training too...to keep still!). Breeders have avoided using Briards with the liver deficiency factor in breeding programmes, and with the advent of complete canine diets, dogs are being fed quality food that contain all the vitamins that are needed.

Professor Bedford is working on the liver defect to work out exactly what is going wrong, and he is hoping to be able to develop a DNA test so it will be possible to check if a dog is carrying the gene for RPED from a blood test, long before there are any disturbances in vision.

STATIONARY NIGHT BLINDNESS
Stationary night blindness is inherited as a recessive illness. This means that the gene for normal sight covers the presence of the faulty gene: normal is dominant to stationary night blindness, stationary night blindness is recessive to normal sight. Research on stationary night blindness is more advanced than that for RPED, because the genetic mutation has been isolated, and there is a test to see if your Briard carries the faulty gene.

Before the genetic test was available, it was impossible to find out if a dog was a carrier until it became the parent of an affected puppy when it was mated to another carrier. Now a simple blood test can tell if your Briard is affected, is a carrier or is clear of the problem. The blood test is an easier examination than the electroretinogram, which is a recording of the eye's electrical response to a flash of light.

An affected Briard will have no vision at night from six weeks of age, but the amount of daylight vision is variable. Some affected dogs will have normal vision in daylight, while others may have mild visual loss and others severe loss of vision despite the daylight.

The reason that this is called stationary night blindness is that the extent of the visual damage is apparent from the age of six weeks, and it does not deteriorate. It was first described in humans in 1831, in France, when a 16-year-old conscript claimed exemption from military service because he could not see in the dark. Unfortunately he was not believed at first, but after a period of service he was re-examined and gained his exemption. His father, grandfather and great-grandfather all had this problem, which was traced back to a butcher, Jean Nougaret, who had been born in 1637. This is the longest known human pedigree of a genetic illness.

The problem with stationary night blindness is with the special cells that pick up light signals. There are two types of receptor cells in the retina of the eye: the rods and the cones. The cones are concerned with colour vision and the rods with vision when there is little light. This is why we cannot see colours properly when it is dark.

In stationary night blindness, the problem is with the rods. When light falls on them, the pigment they contain, rhodopsin or visual purple, is bleached by the light. In a normal retina, it is soon returned to its original form, ready to be bleached by light again. Each time it is bleached, it

RETINAL RECEPTOR CELLS

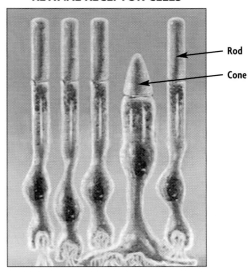

Rod

Cone

sends a signal to the brain, telling it that light is present.

In those with stationary night blindness, this process goes wrong. The rod acts as though it is being constantly bombarded by light, making it no longer sensitive enough to pick up the dim light from things in the dark.

Rhodopsin is made from vitamin A, and vitamin A is derived from carotene as found in carrots. Those with vitamin-A deficiency also suffer from night blindness, so there is some truth in the saying that carrots help you see in the dark. Now that the blood test is easily available, it should be possible to eradicate the genetic form of stationary night blindness from the Briard.

EXTERNAL PARASITES

FLEAS

Of all the problems to which dogs are prone, none is more well known and frustrating than fleas. Flea infestation is relatively simple to cure but difficult to prevent. Parasites that are harboured inside the body are a bit more difficult to eradicate but they are easier to control.

To control flea infestation, you have to understand the flea's life cycle. Fleas are often thought of as a summertime problem, but centrally heated homes have changed the patterns and fleas can be found at any time of the year. The most effective method of flea control is a two-stage approach: one stage to kill the adult fleas, and the other to control the development of pre-adult fleas. Unfortunately, no single active ingredient is effective against all stages of the life cycle.

LIFE CYCLE STAGES

During its life, a flea will pass through four life stages: egg, larva, pupa and adult. The adult stage is the most visible and irritating stage of the flea life cycle, and this is

Magnified head of a dog flea, *Ctenocephalides canis*.

S. E. M. BY DR DENNIS KUNKEL, UNIVERSITY OF HAWAII

Opposite page: A scanning electron micrograph of a dog or cat flea, *Ctenocephalides*, magnified more than 100x. This image has been colorized for effect.

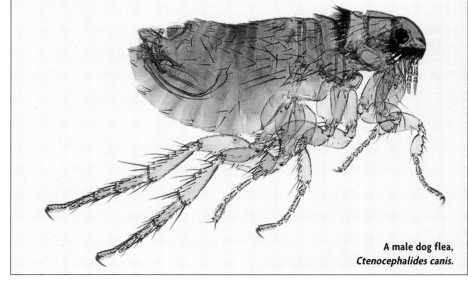

A male dog flea, *Ctenocephalides canis*.

OPPOSITE: S. E. M. BY DR DENNIS KUNKEL, UNIVERSITY OF HAWAII.   PHOTO BY JEAN CLAUDE REVY/PHOTOTAKE

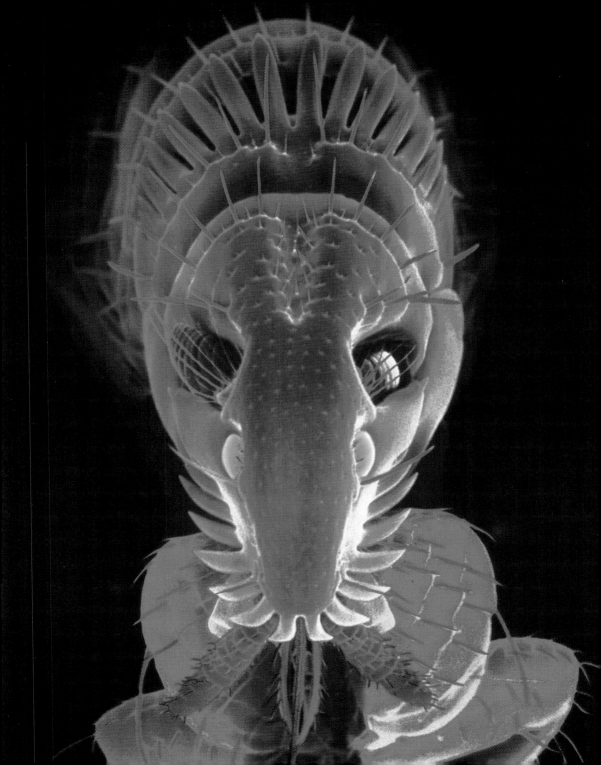

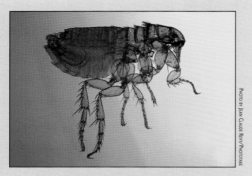

Photo by Jean Claude Revy/Phototake

A LOOK AT FLEAS

Fleas have been around for millions of years and have adapted to changing host animals. They are able to go through a complete life cycle in less than one month or they can extend their lives to almost two years by remaining as pupae or cocoons. They do not need blood or any other food for up to 20 months.

They have been measured as being able to jump 300,000 times and can jump 150 times their length in any direction, including straight up. Those are just a few of the reasons why they are so successful in infesting a dog!

why the majority of flea-control products concentrate on this stage. The fact is that adult fleas account for only 1% of the total flea population, and the other 99% exist in pre-adult stages, i.e. eggs, larvae and pupae. The pre-adult stages are barely visible to the naked eye.

THE LIFE CYCLE OF THE FLEA

Eggs are laid on the dog, usually in quantities of about 20 or 30, several times a day. The female adult flea must have a blood meal before each egg-laying session. When first laid, the eggs will cling to the dog's hair, as the eggs are still moist. However, they will quickly dry out and fall from the dog, especially if the dog moves around or scratches. Many eggs will fall off in the dog's favourite area or an area in which he spends a lot of time, such as his bed.

Once the eggs fall from the dog onto the carpet or furniture, they will hatch into larvae. This takes from one to ten days. Larvae are not particularly mobile and will usually travel only a few inches

The Life Cycle of the Flea

Eggs

Larvae

Pupa

Photo courtesy of Fleabusters Rx for Fleas.

Adult

FLEA KILLERS

Flea-killers are poisonous. You should not spray these toxic chemicals on areas of a dog's body that he licks, on his genitals or on his face. Flea killers taken internally are a better answer, but check with your vet in case internal therapy is not advised for your dog.

INSECT GROWTH REGULATOR (IGR)

Two types of products should be used when treating fleas—a product to treat the pet and a product to treat the home. Adult fleas represent less than 1% of the flea population. The pre-adult fleas (eggs, larvae and pupae) represent more than 99% of the flea population and are found in the environment; it is in the case of pre-adult fleas that products containing an Insect Growth Regulator (IGR) should be used in the home.

IGRs are a new class of compounds used to prevent the development of insects. They do not kill the insect outright, but instead use the insect's biology against it to stop it from completing its growth. Products that contain methoprene are the world's first and leading IGRs. Used to control fleas and other insects, this type of IGR will stop flea larvae from developing and protect the house for up to seven months.

from where they hatch. However, they do have a tendency to move away from light and heavy traffic—under furniture and behind doors are common places to find high quantities of flea larvae.

The flea larvae feed on dead organic matter, including adult flea faeces, until they are ready to change into adult fleas. Fleas will usually remain as larvae for around seven days. After this period, the larvae will pupate into protective pupae. While inside the pupae, the larvae will undergo metamorphosis and change into adult fleas. This can take as little time as a few days, but the adult fleas can remain inside the pupae waiting to hatch for up to two years. The pupae are signalled to hatch by certain stimuli, such as physical pressure—the pupae's being stepped on, heat from an animal lying on the pupae or increased carbon dioxide levels and vibrations—indicating that a suitable host is available.

Once hatched, the adult flea must feed within a few days. Once the adult flea finds an host, it will not leave voluntarily. It only becomes dislodged by grooming or the host animal's scratching. The adult flea will remain on the host for the duration of its life unless forcibly removed.

PHOTO BY DWIGHT R KUHN

Dwight R Kuhn's magnificent action photo, showing a flea jumping from a dog's back.

TREATING THE ENVIRONMENT AND THE DOG

Treating fleas should be a two-pronged attack. First, the environment needs to be treated; this includes carpets and furniture, especially the dog's bedding and areas underneath furniture. The environment should be treated with an household spray containing an Insect Growth Regulator (IGR) and an insecticide to kill the adult fleas. Most IGRs are effective against eggs and

A scanning electron micrograph (S. E. M.) of a dog flea, *Ctenocephalides canis.*

S. E. M. BY DR DENNIS KUNKEL, UNIVERSITY OF HAWAII

EN GARDE: CATCHING FLEAS OFF GUARD!

Consider the following ways to arm yourself against fleas:
• Add a small amount of pennyroyal or eucalyptus oil to your dog's bath. These natural remedies repel fleas.
• Supplement your dog's food with fresh garlic (minced or grated) and an hearty amount of brewer's yeast, both of which ward off fleas.
• Use a flea comb on your dog daily. Submerge fleas in a cup of bleach to kill them quickly.
• Confine the dog to only a few rooms to limit the spread of fleas in the home.
• Vacuum daily...and get all of the crevices! Dispose of the bag every few days until the problem is under control.
• Wash your dog's bedding daily. Cover cushions where your dog sleeps with towels, and wash the towels often.

larvae; they actually mimic the fleas' own hormones and stop the eggs and larvae from developing into adult fleas. There are currently no treatments available to attack the pupa stage of the life cycle, so the adult insecticide is used to kill the newly hatched adult fleas before they find an host. Most IGRs are active for many months, while adult insecticides are only active for a few days.

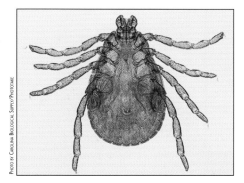

A brown dog tick, *Rhipicephalus sanguineus*, is an uncommon but annoying tick found on dogs.

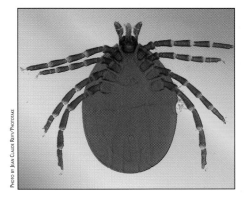

An uncommon dog tick of the genus *Ixode*. Magnified 10x.

When treating with an household spray, it is a good idea to vacuum before applying the product. This stimulates as many pupae as possible to hatch into adult fleas. The vacuum cleaner should also be treated with an insecticide to prevent the eggs and larvae that have been hoovered into the vacuum bag from hatching.

The second stage of treatment is to apply an adult insecticide to the dog. Traditionally, this would be in the form of a collar or a spray, but more recent innovations include digestible insecticides that poison the fleas when they ingest the dog's blood. Alternatively, there are drops that, when placed on the back of the animal's neck, spread throughout the fur and skin to kill adult fleas.

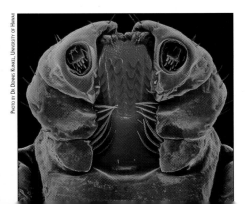

TICKS AND MITES

Though not as common as fleas, ticks and mites are found all over the tropical and temperate world. They don't bite, like fleas; they harpoon. They dig their sharp proboscis (nose) into the dog's skin and drink the blood. Their only food and drink is dog's blood. Dogs can get Lyme disease, Rocky Mountain spotted fever (normally found in the US only), paralysis and many other diseases from ticks and mites. They may live where fleas are

The head of a dog tick, *Dermacentor variabilis*, enlarged and coloured for effect.

The mange mite, *Psoroptes bovis.*

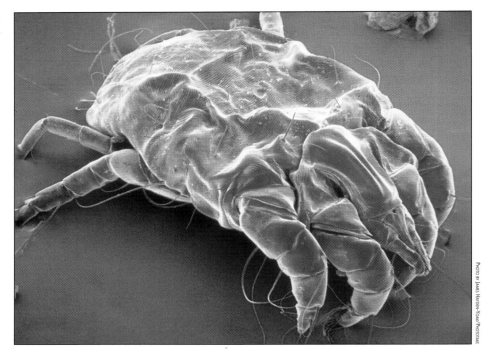

PHOTO BY JAMES HAYDEN-YOAV/PHOTOTAKE

The roundworm, *Rhabditis.* The roundworm can infect both dogs and humans.

PHOTO BY CAROLINA BIOLOGICAL SUPPLY/PHOTOTAKE

The common roundworm, *Ascaris lumbricoides.*

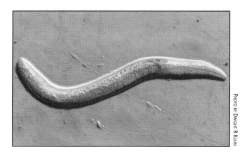

PHOTO BY DWIGHT R KUHN

administered by a vet, followed by Tresaderm at home.

It is essential that your dog be treated for mange as quickly as possible because some forms of mange are transmissible to people.

INTERNAL PARASITES

Most animals—fishes, birds and mammals, including dogs and humans—have worms and other parasites that live inside their bodies. According to Dr Herbert R Axelrod, the fish pathologist, there are two kinds of parasites: dumb and smart. The smart parasites live in peaceful cooperation with their hosts (symbiosis),

while the dumb parasites kill
their hosts. Most of the worm
infections are relatively easy to
control. If they are not controlled,
they weaken the host dog to the
point that other medical problems
occur, but they are not dumb
parasites.

ROUNDWORMS

The roundworms that infect dogs
are scientifically known as
Toxocara canis. They live in the
dog's intestines. The worms shed
eggs continually. It has been
estimated that a dog produces
about 150 grammes of faeces
every day. Each gramme of faeces

ROUNDWORMS

Average size dogs can pass
1,360,000 roundworm eggs every
day. For example, if there were only
1 million dogs in the world, the
world would be saturated with
1,300 metric tonnes of dog faeces.
These faeces would contain
15,000,000,000 roundworm eggs.

Up to 31% of home gardens and
children's play boxes in the US
contain roundworm eggs.

Flushing dog's faeces down the
toilet is not a safe practice because
the usual sewage treatments do not
destroy roundworm eggs.

Infected puppies start shedding
roundworm eggs at 3 weeks of age.
They can be infected by their
mother's milk.

DEWORMING

Ridding your puppy of worms is
very important because certain
worms that puppies carry, such as
tapeworms and roundworms, can
infect humans.

Breeders initiate deworming
programmes at or about four weeks
of age. The routine is repeated
every two or three weeks until the
puppy is three months old. The
breeder from whom you obtained
your puppy should provide you with
the complete details of the
deworming programme.

Your veterinary surgeon can
prescribe and monitor the
programme of deworming for you.
The usual programme is treating the
puppy every 15–20 days until the
puppy is positively worm-free. It is
advised that you only treat your
puppy with drugs that are
recommended professionally.

---

averages 10,000–12,000 eggs of
roundworms. There are no
known areas in which dogs roam
that do not contain roundworm
eggs. The greatest danger of
roundworms is that they infect
people too! It is wise to have
your dog tested regularly for
roundworms.

Pigs also have roundworm
infections that can be passed to
humans and dogs. The typical
roundworm parasite is called
Ascaris lumbricoides.

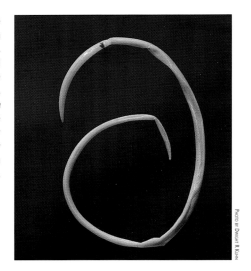

PHOTO BY DWIGHT R KUHN

Left: The roundworm *Rhabditis*. Right: Male and female hookworms. *Ancylostoma caninum* are uncommonly found in pet or show dogs in Britain.

The infective stage of the hookworm larva.

HOOKWORMS

The worm *Ancylostoma caninum* is commonly called the dog hookworm. It is also dangerous to humans and cats. It has teeth by which it attaches itself to the intestines of the dog. It changes the site of its attachment about six times a day and the dog loses blood from each detachment, possibly causing iron-deficiency anaemia. Hookworms are easily purged from the dog with many medications. Milbemycin oxime, which also serves as an heartworm preventative in Collies, can be used for this purpose.

In Britain the 'temperate climate' hookworm (*Uncinaria stenocephala*) is rarely found in pet or show dogs, but can occur in hunting packs, racing Greyhounds and sheepdogs because the worms can be prevalent wherever dogs are exercised regularly on grassland.

TAPEWORMS

There are many species of tapeworm. They are carried by fleas! The dog eats the flea and starts the tapeworm cycle. Humans can also be infected with tapeworms, so don't eat fleas! Fleas are so small that your dog could pass them onto your hands, your plate or your food and thus make it possible for you to ingest a flea that is carrying tapeworm eggs.

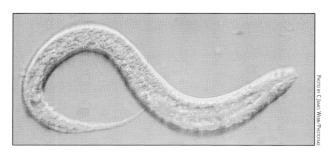

PHOTO BY C JAMES WEBB/PHOTOTAKE

Heartworm,
Dirofilaria immitis.

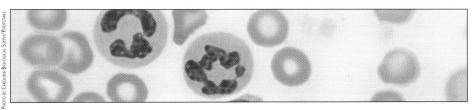

Magnified
heartworm larvae,
Dirofilaria immitis.

While tapeworm infection is not life-threatening in dogs (smart parasite!), it can be the cause of a very serious liver disease for humans. About 50 percent of the humans infected with *Echinococcus multilocularis,* a type of tapeworm that causes alveolar hydatis, perish.

TAPEWORMS

Humans, rats, squirrels, foxes, coyotes, wolves and domestic dogs are all susceptible to tapeworm infection. Except in humans, tapeworms are usually not a fatal infection. Infected individuals can harbour a thousand parasitic worms.

Tapeworms have two sexes—male and female (many other worms have only one sex—male and female in the same worm).

If dogs eat infected rats or mice, they get the tapeworm disease. One month after attaching to a dog's intestine, the worm starts shedding eggs. These eggs are infective immediately. Infective eggs can live for a few months without an host animal.

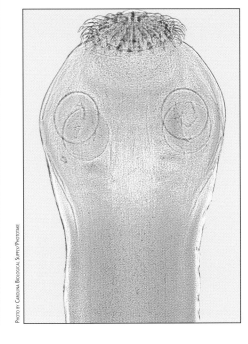

The head and rostellum (the round prominence on the scolex) of a tapeworm, which infects dogs and humans.

PHOTO BY JAMES E HANKIN, RPB/PHOTOTAKE

HEARTWORMS

Heartworms are thin, extended worms up to 30 cms (12 ins) long, which live in a dog's heart and the major blood vessels surrounding it. Dogs may have up to 200 worms. Symptoms may be loss of energy, loss of appetite, coughing, the development of a potbelly and anaemia.

Heartworms are transmitted by mosquitoes. The mosquito drinks the blood of an infected dog and takes in larvae with the blood. The larvae, called microfilaria, develop within the body of the mosquito and are passed on to the next dog bitten after the larvae mature. It takes two to three weeks for the larvae to develop to the infective stage within the body of the mosquito. Dogs should be treated at about six weeks of age, and maintained on a prophylactic dose given monthly.

Blood testing for heartworms is not necessarily indicative of how seriously your dog is infected. This is a dangerous disease. Although heartworm is a problem for dogs in America, Australia, Asia and Central Europe, dogs in the United Kingdom are not currently affected by heartworm.

First Aid at a Glance

Burns
Place the affected area under cool water;
use ice if only a small area is burnt.

Bee/Insect bites
Apply ice to relieve swelling;
antihistamine dosed properly.

Animal bites
Clean any bleeding area; apply pressure
until bleeding subsides; go to the vet.

Spider bites
Use cold compress and a pressurised
pack to inhibit venom's spreading.

Antifreeze poisoning
Induce vomiting with hydrogen peroxide.
Seek *immediate* veterinary help!

Fish hooks
Removal best handled by vet;
hook must be cut in order to remove.

Snake bites
Pack ice around bite; contact vet
quickly; identify snake for proper
antivenin.

Car accident
Move dog from roadway with blanket;
seek veterinary aid.

Shock
Calm the dog, keep him warm; seek
immediate veterinary help.

Nosebleed
Apply cold compress to the nose; apply
pressure to any visible abrasion.

Bleeding
Apply pressure above the area; treat
wound by applying a cotton pack.

Heat stroke
Submerge dog in cold bath; cool down
with fresh air and water; go to the vet.

Frostbite/Hypothermia
Warm the dog with a warm bath, electric
blankets or hot water bottles.

Abrasions
Clean the wound and wash out
thoroughly with fresh water;
apply antiseptic.

 *Remember: an injured dog may attempt
to bite a helping hand from fear and confusion.
Always muzzle the dog before trying to offer assistance.*

HOMEOPATHY:
an alternative
to conventional
medicine

'Less is Most'

Using this principle, the strength of a homeopathic remedy is measured by the number of serial dilutions that were undertaken to create it. The greater the number of serial dilutions, the greater the strength of the homeopathic remedy. The potency of a remedy that has been made by making a dilution of 1 part in 100 parts (or 1/100) is 1c or 1cH. If this remedy is subjected to a series of further dilutions, each one being 1/100, a more dilute and stronger remedy is produced. If the remedy is diluted in this way six times, it is called 6c or 6cH. A dilution of 6c is 1 part in 1,000,000,000,000. In general, higher potencies in more frequent doses are better for acute symptoms and lower potencies in more infrequent doses are more useful for chronic, long-standing problems.

CURING OUR DOGS NATURALLY

Holistic medicine means treating the whole animal as a unique, perfect living being. Generally, holistic treatments do not suppress the symptoms that the body naturally produces, as do most medications prescribed by conventional doctors and vets. Holistic methods seek to cure disease by regaining balance and harmony in the patient's environment. Some of these methods include use of nutritional therapy, herbs, flower essences, aromatherapy, acupuncture, massage, chiropractic and, of course, the most popular holistic approach, homeopathy.

Homeopathy is a theory or system of treating illness with small doses of substances which, if administered in larger quantities, would produce the symptoms that the patient already has. This approach is often described as 'like cures like.' Although modern veterinary medicine is geared toward the 'quick fix,' homeopathy relies on the belief that, given the time, the body is able to heal itself and return to its natural, healthy state.

Choosing a remedy to cure a problem in our dogs is the difficult part of homeopathy. Consult with your veterinary surgeon for a professional diagnosis of your dog's symptoms. Often these symptoms require immediate conventional care. If your vet is willing, and knowledgeable, you may attempt a homeopathic remedy. Be aware that cortisone prevents homeopathic remedies from working. There are hundreds of possibilities and combinations to cure many problems in dogs, from basic physical problems such as excessive moulting, fleas, obesity or other parasites, unattractive doggy odour, bad breath, upset tummy, dry, oily or dull coat, diarrhoea, ear problems or eye discharge (including tears and dry or mucousy matter), to behavioural abnormalities, such as fear of loud noises, habitual licking, poor appetite, excessive barking, and various phobias. From alumina to zincum metallicum, the remedies span the planet and the imagination…from flowers and weeds to chemicals, insect droppings, diesel smoke and volcanic ash.

Using 'Like to Treat Like'

Unlike conventional medicines that suppress symptoms, homeopathic remedies treat illnesses with small doses of substances that, if administered in larger quantities, would produce the symptoms that the patient already has. While the same homeopathic remedy can be used to treat different symptoms in different dogs, here are some interesting remedies and their uses.

Apis Mellifica
(made from honey bee venom) can be used for allergies or to reduce swelling that occurs in acutely infected kidneys.

Diesel Smoke
can be used to help control travel sickness.

Calcarea Fluorica
(made from calcium fluoride, which helps harden bone structure) can be useful in treating hard lumps in tissues.

Natrum Muriaticum
(made from common salt, sodium chloride) is useful in treating thin, thirsty dogs.

Nitricum Acidum
(made from nitric acid) is used for symptoms you would expect to see from contact with acids, such as lesions, especially where the skin joins the linings of body orifices or openings such as the lips and nostrils.

Symphytum
(made from the herb Knitbone, *Symphytum officianale*) is used to encourage bones to heal.

Urtica Urens
(made from the common stinging nettle) is used in treating painful, irritating rashes.

HOMEOPATHIC REMEDIES FOR YOUR DOG

Symptom/Ailment	Possible Remedy
ALLERGIES	Apis Mellifica 30c, Astacus Fluviatilis 6c, Pulsatilla 30c, Urtica Urens 6c
ALOPAECIA	Alumina 30c, Lycopodium 30c, Sepia 30c, Thallium 6c
ANAL GLANDS (BLOCKED)	Hepar Sulphuris Calcareum 30c, Sanicula 6c, Silicea 6c
ARTHRITIS	Rhus Toxicodendron 6c, Bryonia Alba 6c
CATARACT	Calcarea Carbonica 6c, Conium Maculatum 6c, Phosphorus 30c, Silicea 30c
CONSTIPATION	Alumina 6c, Carbo Vegetabilis 30c, Graphites 6c, Nitricum Acidum 30c, Silicea 6c
COUGHING	Aconitum Napellus 6c, Belladonna 30c, Hyoscyamus Niger 30c, Phosphorus 30c
DIARRHOEA	Arsenicum Album 30c, Aconitum Napellus 6c, Chamomilla 30c, Mercurius Corrosivus 30c
DRY EYE	Zincum Metallicum 30c
EAR PROBLEMS	Aconitum Napellus 30c, Belladonna 30c, Hepar Sulphuris 30c, Tellurium 30c, Psorinum 200c
EYE PROBLEMS	Borax 6c, Aconitum Napellus 30c, Graphites 6c, Staphysagria 6c, Thuja Occidentalis 30c
GLAUCOMA	Aconitum Napellus 30c, Apis Mellifica 6c, Phosphorus 30c
HEAT STROKE	Belladonna 30c, Gelsemium Sempervirens 30c, Sulphur 30c
HICCOUGHS	Cinchona Deficinalis 6c
HIP DYSPLASIA	Colocynthis 6c, Rhus Toxicodendron 6c, Bryonia Alba 6c
INCONTINENCE	Argentum Nitricum 6c, Causticum 30c, Conium Maculatum 30c, Pulsatilla 30c, Sepia 30c
INSECT BITES	Apis Mellifica 30c, Cantharis 30c, Hypericum Perforatum 6c, Urtica Urens 30c
ITCHING	Alumina 30c, Arsenicum Album 30c, Carbo Vegetabilis 30c, Hypericum Perforatum 6c, Mezerium 6c, Sulphur 30c
KENNEL COUGH	Drosera 6c, Ipecacuanha 30c
MASTITIS	Apis Mellifica 30c, Belladonna 30c, Urtica Urens 1m
PATELLAR LUXATION	Gelsemium Sempervirens 6c, Rhus Toxicodendron 6c
PENIS PROBLEMS	Aconitum Napellus 30c, Hepar Sulphuris Calcareum 30c, Pulsatilla 30c, Thuja Occidentalis 6c
PUPPY TEETHING	Calcarea Carbonica 6c, Chamomilla 6c, Phytolacca 6c
TRAVEL SICKNESS	Cocculus 6c, Petroleum 6c

Recognising a Sick Dog

Unlike colicky babies and cranky children, our canine kids cannot tell us when they are feeling ill. Therefore, there are a number of signs that owners can identify to know that their dogs are not feeling well.

Take note for physical manifestations such as:

- unusual, bad odour, including bad breath
- excessive moulting
- wax in the ears, chronic ear irritation
- oily, flaky, dull haircoat
- mucous, tearing or similar discharge in the eyes
- fleas or mites
- mucous in stool, diarrhoea
- sensitivity to petting or handling
- licking at paws, scratching face, etc.

Keep an eye out for behavioural changes as well including:

- lethargy, idleness
- lack of patience or general irritability
- lack of appetite, digestive problems
- phobias (fear of people, loud noises, etc.)
- strange behaviour, suspicion, fear
- coprophagia
- more frequent barking
- whimpering, crying

Get Well Soon

You don't need a DVR or a BVMA to provide good TLC to your sick or recovering dog, but you do need to pay attention to some details that normally wouldn't bother him. The following tips will aid Fido's recovery and get him back on his paws again:

- Keep his space free of irritating smells, like heavy perfumes and air fresheners.
- Rest is the best medicine! Avoid harsh lighting that will prevent your dog from sleeping. Shade him from bright sunlight during the day and dim the lights in the evening.
- Keep the noise level down. Animals are more sensitive to sound when they are sick.

- Be attentive to any necessary temperature adjustments. A dog with a fever needs a cool room and cold liquids. A bitch that is whelping or recovering from surgery will be more comfortable in a warm room, consuming warm liquids and food.
- You wouldn't send a sick child back to school early, so don't rush your dog back into a full routine until he seems absolutely ready.

Number-One Killer Disease in Dogs: CANCER

In every age there is a word associated with a disease or plague that causes humans to shudder. In the 21st century, that word is 'cancer.' Just as cancer is the leading cause of death in humans, it claims nearly half the lives of dogs that die from a natural disease as well as half the dogs that die over the age of ten years.

Described as a genetic disease, cancer becomes a greater risk as the dog ages. Veterinary surgeons and dog owners have become increasingly aware of the threat of cancer to dogs. Statistics reveal that one dog in every five will develop cancer, the most common of which is skin cancer. Many cancers, including prostate, ovarian and breast cancer, can be avoided by spaying and neutering our dogs by the age of six months.

Early detection of cancer can save or extend your dog's life, so it is absolutely vital for owners to have their dogs examined by a qualified veterinary surgeon or oncologist immediately upon detection of any abnormality. Certain dietary guidelines have also proven to reduce the onset and spread of cancer. Foods based on fish rather than beef, due to the presence of Omega-3 fatty acids, are recommended. Other amino acids such as glutamine have significant benefits for canines, particularly those breeds that show a greater susceptibility to cancer.

Cancer management and treatments promise hope for future generations of canines. Since the disease is genetic, breeders should never breed a dog whose parents, grandparents and any related siblings have developed cancer. It is difficult to know whether to exclude an otherwise healthy dog from a breeding programme as the disease does not manifest itself until the dog's senior years.

RECOGNISE CANCER WARNING SIGNS

Since early detection can possibly rescue your dog from becoming a cancer statistic, it is essential for owners to recognise the possible signs and seek the assistance of a qualified professional.

- Abnormal bumps or lumps that continue to grow
- Bleeding or discharge from any body cavity
- Persistent stiffness or lameness
- Recurrent sores or sores that do not heal
- Inappetence
- Breathing difficulties
- Weight loss
- Bad breath or odours
- General malaise and fatigue
- Eating and swallowing problems
- Difficulty urinating and defecating

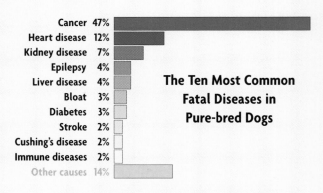

Cancer	47%
Heart disease	12%
Kidney disease	7%
Epilepsy	4%
Liver disease	4%
Bloat	3%
Diabetes	3%
Stroke	2%
Cushing's disease	2%
Immune diseases	2%
Other causes	14%

The Ten Most Common Fatal Diseases in Pure-bred Dogs

CDS: COGNITIVE DYSFUNCTION SYNDROME

'OLD-DOG SYNDROME'

There are many ways to evaluate old-dog syndrome. Veterinary surgeons have defined CDS (cognitive dysfunction syndrome) as the gradual deterioration of cognitive abilities. These are indicated by changes in the dog's behaviour. When a dog changes its routine response, and maladies have been eliminated as the cause of these behavioural changes, then CDS is the usual diagnosis.

More than half the dogs over eight years old suffer from some form of CDS. The older the dog, the more chance it has of suffering from CDS. In humans, doctors often dismiss the CDS behavioural changes as part of 'winding down.'

There are four major signs of CDS: the dog has frequent toilet accidents inside the home, sleeps much more or much less than normal, acts confused and fails to respond to social stimuli.

SYMPTOMS OF CDS

FREQUENT TOILET ACCIDENTS
- *Urinates in the house.*
- *Defecates in the house.*
- *Doesn't signal that he wants to go out.*

SLEEP PATTERNS
- *Moves much more slowly.*
- *Sleeps more than normal during the day.*
- *Sleeps less during the night.*

CONFUSION
- *Goes outside and just stands there.*
- *Appears confused with a faraway look in his eyes.*
- *Hides more often.*
- *Doesn't recognise friends.*
- *Doesn't come when called.*
- *Walks around listlessly and without a destination.*

FAILS TO RESPOND TO SOCIAL STIMULI
- *Comes to people less frequently, whether called or not.*
- *Doesn't tolerate petting for more than a short time.*
- *Doesn't come to the door when you return home.*

BRIARD

The term *old* is a qualitative term. For dogs, as well as their masters, old is relative. Certainly we can all distinguish between a Briard puppy and adult—there are the obvious physical traits such as size, facial appearance and also the personality traits. Puppies that are nasty are rare. Puppies and young dogs like to play with children, and a child's natural exuberance is a good match for the periods of energy of a young dog. They like to run, jump and chase. As an adult, the Briard will retain many of these juvenile behaviour patterns until it is really getting quite elderly.

On the other hand, if a Briard is only exposed to people over 60 years of age, its life will normally be less active so there will not be as great a change and it will not seem to be getting old as its activity level slows down.

All breeds of dog have to be considered individually when it comes to considering their ageing process. A small breed like a Shih Tzu may live to 20 years, larger breeds are considered seniors by the age of 8, and giant breeds like the Great Dane are very elderly indeed at 10 years old. The average lifespan of a Briard is 11 years.

WHAT TO LOOK FOR IN SENIORS

Most veterinary surgeons and indeed the dog show world use the seven-year mark as the time to consider a dog as a veteran. Ageing is essentially a slowing process. Humans readily admit they feel a difference in their activity level from age 20 to 30, and then from 30 to 40. By treating the seven-year-old dog as a senior, owners are able to implement certain therapeutic and preventative medical strategies with the help of their veterinary surgeons. A senior-care programme should include at least two veterinary visits a year, screening sessions to determine the health status, as well as nutritional counselling.

Such a programme for senior dogs is well advised before owners start to see the obvious physical signs of ageing, such as slower and inhibited movement, greying, increased sleep/nap periods and disinterest in play and other activity. This preventative programme helps to give a longer, healthier life for the ageing dog. Among the physical problems common in ageing dogs are the loss of sight and hearing, kidney and liver failure, diabetes mellitus and heart disease.

In addition to these physical problems, there are also behavioural changes and problems in relation to ageing dogs. Dogs suffering from hearing or visual loss, dental discomfort or arthritis can become aggressive. Likewise, the near- deaf and/or blind dog may be startled more easily and react in an uncharacteristically aggressive manner. Seniors suffering from senility can become more impatient and irritable. Housesoiling accidents are associated with loss of mobility, kidney problems, loss of sphincter control, brain changes and perhaps reaction to medication.

Older dogs, just like puppies, suffer from separation anxiety, which can lead to excessive barking, whining, housesoiling and destructive behaviour. Seniors may become fearful of everyday sounds, such as vacuum cleaners, heaters, thunder and passing traffic. Some dogs have difficulty sleeping, due to discomfort, the need for frequent potty visits and the like.

Owners should avoid spoiling the older dog with too many fatty treats. Keep the senior dog as trim as possible, because as activity lessens it is easier for your Briard to become obese. It is possible to get speciality diets for senior dogs, but these do not taste as nice as the higher fat diets and the older Briard can reject them.

Your dog, as he nears his twilight years, needs your patience and care more than ever. Never punish an older dog for an accident or abnormal behaviour. He deserves special attention and

Among the signs that your Briard has slowed down is his increased sleep periods and general decrease in activity.

courtesies for all the years of love, companionship and protection that he has provided. The older dog may need to relieve himself at 3 a.m. because he can no longer hold his urine for eight hours. He will appreciate the consideration that you offer as he gets older.

Your Briard does not understand why is world is slowing down. You must make the transition into the golden years as pleasant and rewarding as possible.

WHAT TO DO WHEN THE TIME COMES
You are never fully prepared to make a rational decision about putting your dog to sleep. It is very obvious that you care about your Briard or you would not be reading this book. Putting a loved dog to sleep is extremely difficult. It is a decision that must be made with your veterinary surgeon. You are usually forced to make the decision when one of the life-threatening symptoms listed above becomes serious enough for you to seek veterinary help.

If the prognosis indicates the end is near, and your beloved pet will only suffer more, and experience no enjoyment for the rest of his life, then euthanasia is the right choice.

WHAT IS EUTHANASIA?
Euthanasia derives from the Greek, meaning *good death*. In other

EUTHANASIA
Euthanasia must be performed by a licensed veterinary surgeon. There also may be societies for the prevention of cruelty to animals in your area. They often offer this service upon a vet's recommendation.

words, it means the planned, painless killing of a dog suffering from a painful, incurable condition, or who is so aged that he cannot walk, see, eat or control his excretory functions.

Euthanasia is usually carried out by an injection that is an overdose of anaesthetic or barbiturate. Aside from the prick of the needle, the experience is usually painless.

MAKING THE DECISION
The decision to euthanize is never easy. The days during which the dog becomes ill, and when the end comes can be unusually stressful for you. If this is your first experience of the death of a loved one, you may need the comfort dictated by your religious beliefs. The whole family should be involved in the decision to put your Briard to sleep. If your dog is being maintained on drugs, this will give you time to make a decision. During this time, talking with members of your family or people who have lived through this experience can help ease the

burden of your inevitable decision.

THE FINAL RESTING PLACE

Dogs can have some of the same privileges as humans. They can occasionally be buried in a pet cemetery, which is generally expensive, or they can be cremated and the ashes returned to place in the garden, perhaps to be marked with a stone or a newly planted tree or bush. In Britain there are regulations to prevent pet burial in your garden. Some people prefer to leave the body with their vet.

All of these options should be discussed with your veterinary surgeon. Do not be afraid to ask financial questions. Cremations can be individual, but a less expensive option is cremation with others, although of course then the ashes cannot be returned. Vets can usually arrange cremation on your behalf. You must be aware that in Britain if you dog has died at the surgery the vet cannot legally allow you to take your dog's body home.

GETTING ANOTHER DOG?

The grief of losing your beloved dog will be as lasting as the grief of losing a human friend or relative. In most cases, if your dog died of old age, it had slowed down considerably. Do you want a new Briard puppy to replace it? Or are you better off finding a more mature Briard, say two to three years of age, which will usually be house-trained and will have an already developed personality. In this case you can find out if you like each other after a few hours of being together.

The decision is, of course, your own. Do you want another Briard or perhaps a different breed so as to avoid comparison with your beloved friend? Most people usually buy the same breed because they know (and love) the characteristics of that breed. Then, too, they often know people who have the same breed and perhaps they are lucky enough that a breeder they know and respect expects a litter that will be related to their lost pet and should share many of his characteristics.

SENIOR SIGNS

An old dog starts to show one or more of the following symptoms:

- The hair on the face and paws starts to turn grey. The colour breakdown usually starts around the eyes and mouth.

- Sleep patterns are deeper and longer, and the old dog is harder to awaken.

- Food intake diminishes.

- Responses to calls, whistles and other signals are ignored more and more.

- Eye contact does not evoke tail wagging (assuming it once did).

Showing Your
BRIARD

When you purchase your Briard, you will make it clear to the breeder whether you want one as a loveable companion and pet, or if you hoped to be buying a Briard with show prospects. No reputable breeder will sell you a young puppy saying that it is *definitely* of show quality, for so much can go wrong during the early weeks and months of a puppy's development. If you plan to show, what you will hopefully have acquired is a puppy with 'show potential.'

To the novice, exhibiting a Briard in the show ring may look easy but it takes a lot of hard work and dedication to do top winning at a show such as the prestigious Crufts, not to mention a little luck too.

The first concept that the canine novice learns when watching a dog show is that each breed first competes against members of its own breed. At most shows, the group system is used, and once the judge has selected the best member of each breed, that chosen dog will compete with the other dogs in its group. The Briard is in the Pastoral Group in Britain, where it competes with breeds like the Old English Sheepdog, Rough Collie and Belgian Shepherd Dog. In those countries that use Fédération Cynologique Internationale (FCI) rules, which is most of the rest of the world with the exception of the United States, the Briard is in Group One, which is very similar to the Pastoral Group. Once the winners of each of the seven British or ten FCI groups have been chosen, they compete with each other for the award of Best in Show.

The second concept that you must understand is that the dogs are not actually compared against one another. The judge compares each dog against the breed standard, the written description of the ideal specimen of the breed, which we have discussed earlier. While some early breed standards were indeed based on specific dogs that were deemed outstanding when the breed was in the early stages of develop-ment, it is more accurate to say that the perfect specimen, as described by the standard, has never been bred. Thus the 'perfect' dog has never walked into a show ring, has never been bred from and, to the woe of dog breeders around the globe, does not exist. Breeders attempt to get as close to this ideal as possible, with every litter, but theoretically the 'perfect' dog is so elusive that it is impossible. (And if the 'perfect' dog were born, breeders and judges would never agree that it was indeed 'perfect.')

If you are interested in exploring dog shows, it may be that there is a local breed club. In Britain there are two clubs for the Briard: the Briard Association and the British Briard Club. In Europe the norm is one breed club per country. There are several clubs for Briard in the United States, as this is a large country; in Britain, popular breeds have numerous breed clubs as well. Both of the British Briard breed clubs hold Championship Shows, where it is possible to win awards towards the title of Champion, and they also hold the slightly less prestigious Open Shows. The clubs also hold special events and small shows just for club members, all of which could be of interest, even if you are only an onlooker. The clubs also send out newsletters and organise training days and seminars in order that people may learn more about the Briard. The Kennel Club can give you the addresses of the secretaries of the two Briard clubs in Britain.

The Kennel Club is in charge of dog showing in Britain, ensuring that its rules are obeyed and doing what it can to promote the world of pedigreed dogs. As well as conformation shows, The Kennel Club is also in charge of working trials, obedience shows, agility trials and field trials. The Kennel Club furnishes the rules and regulations for all of these events, plus general dog registration. It came into being in 1873 when the show ring was a hotbed of deceit and when one dog was substituted for another; for example, 40 Pointers had the name 'Bob' because the original Bob was a big show winner. One of The Kennel Club's first tasks was to set up the registration system, and to publish the real wins of dogs (no trades description legislation in advertisements then) so that individual dogs could be differentiated from each other.

The Kennel Club holds its own show, Crufts, annually, and this is the largest dog show in the world with more than 20,000 entries each year. British dog shows are the largest in the world, due to the high density of show dogs in what is really a small country. The average all-breed entry at an American show with championship points on offer for all breeds is about 1000 dogs, with some big shows with an entry of double this, and the very largest going on to 4000 entries.

The most prestigious American show is that run by the Westminster Kennel Club, held in New York in February each year. This show started in 1877, and is the longest-running show in the world, as the British and European shows were forced to break by the events of two World Wars. Until 1992 the entries were limited to the first 2000 through the post, but since then it has been the first 2000 champions to apply for entry.

A British dog needs to win best of its sex at three Championship Shows, with three different judges adjudicating, to gain the title of Champion. This is the hardest title to win anywhere in the world. Not only are there usually the highest number of entries, but the prospective champion has to be best of sex over all the dogs that have already gained their championship title. In the United States, for example, any dog with a championship title goes into a separate class and only competes for Best of Breed. So the 'Winners Dog' may win championship points for being the best non-titled male present, but may not be the best male there at all.

The winner of best of sex at a British championship show wins a certificate formally known as a Challenge Certificate (CC), also called a ticket.

In Britain, the number of dogs competing does not affect the worth of the best of sex award; high standards are maintained by the withholding of awards if no dog of sufficient merit is present. In the United States, there are complex tables created by the American Kennel Club to reflect the geographical popularity of each breed. This means that each 'best of non-titled of that sex' has a different point value. Fifteen points are needed for an American title, and the maximum available at a very large show is 5. A win of 3, 4 or 5 points is called a major, and the prospective title-holder must win two majors under two different judges.

In FCI countries, the title of Champion is gained by winning certificates called *Certificats d'Aptitude au Championnat* (CACs) for a national championship, or *Certificats d' Aptitude au Championnat International de Beaute* (CACIBs) for an international title. If there is no dog worthy of the certificate, continental judges withhold the award.

There are three types of British Championship Shows: General Championship Shows, for all Kennel-Club-recognised breeds; Group Championship Shows, limited to breeds within a group; and Breed Championship Shows, such as those limited to Briards alone.

Open Shows are generally less competitive as there are no CCs on offer, and they are often used as 'practice shows' for young dogs. There are hundreds of Open Shows held each year all over Britain, and they are great first-show experiences for the novice.

While Championship and Open Shows are the most important for the beginner to understand, there are other types of British shows as well. Training clubs sponsor Matches that can be entered on the day of the show for a nominal fee. In these introductory-level exhibitions, the names of two dogs are pulled out of the hat and 'matched.' The winner of that match goes on to the next round, and eventually only one dog is left undefeated.

Exemption Shows are much more light-hearted affairs with usually only four pedigreed classes and several 'fun' classes, all of which can be entered on the day of the show. The proceeds of an Exemption Show are given to a charity, and they are sometimes held in conjunctions with fairs or village shows. Limited Shows are those restricted to the members of a club, though it is often possible to join the club when making an entry.

Stepping into the ring can be a very frightening experience, so it is a very good idea to sit back and observe what is happening. The male puppy classes go first,

so if you have a male puppy, it is certainly a good idea to go to a show that you have not entered to see what goes on before starting your career as an exhibitor.

For your first time in the ring, try to be at the end of the line of exhibitors so that you can watch what the judge is asking the others to do. It is much better to stand back and study how the exhibitor in front of you is performing.

The judge will look at all the exhibits in the line and then will ask each exhibitor to come forward in turn to evaluate each dog individually. You will have to step forward when it is your turn and stand your dog, hopefully showing it off to its best advantage. The judge will observe the dog, and then approach to

Attending an outdoor all-breed or speciality show can be an exciting experience for newcomers. You will learn much about how shows work and also more about the Briard.

A Briard manoeuvring through the weave poles at an agility trial.

check the teeth, the anatomical structure of the skeleton and the musculature, all the time considering how well the dog conforms to the breed standard. Most importantly, the judge will have the exhibitor move the dog around the ring in a pattern that he or she will specify (another

advantage of not going first, but always listen since some judges change their directions, and the judge is always right). Finally the judge will give the dog one last look before going on to the next exhibitor.

If you do not win anything at your first show, do not be discouraged. Be patient and, if your dog is good enough, you may eventually find yourself in the winning lineup. Remember that the winners were once in your shoes and have devoted many hours to earn their placement. If you find that your dog is losing every time and never getting a nod, it may be time to consider just enjoying your Briard as a pet.

Judges have varying amounts of knowledge about Briards and unfortunately it is often the ignorance of the judges and/or exhibitors that keeps them turning up at shows. It is frighteningly frequent that ignorance of soundness and true Briard type generates a lottery in which almost anyone will have his day and come home with a prize. As the head is so covered in hair, some do not spend any time trying to learn the correct structure that should be found underneath.

The bar jump is an event at obedience shows, where Briards are capable of performing quite marvellously.

OTHER FORMS OF COMPETITION
There are other forms of shows, working trials, field trials and

The Briard awaits his handler's signal to approach the bar jump.

agility trials. Briards are quite capable of success at agility and working trials to quite a high level. Their natural exuberance will help them sail high over the agility jumps but is perhaps a little of a problem at the timed 'down' in the middle of the course. With a lot of work, they have the mental capability for obedience as well. The newest form of dog sport, flyball, whereby a dog has to cross the course, press the button to release a ball into the air, catch the ball and return to base, is also just up their street. To compete in these events, it is necessary to join a specialist club so that both you and the dog will be fully trained.

The pipe tunnel is a favourite obstacle at agility trials.

My Briard

PUT YOUR PUPPY'S FIRST PICTURE HERE

Dog's Name _____

Date _____ Photographer _____